WO
CHANGERS

FASCINATING FIGURES FROM CHURCH HISTORY

MARTIN LUTHER • GEORGE WISHART • JOHN KNOX

ROBERT MURRAY MCCHEYNE • DAVID LIVINGSTONE

JOHN BUNYAN • JOHN WESLEY • C. H. SPURGEON

HERBERT
LOCKYER

WHITAKER
HOUSE

WORLD CHANGERS:
Fascinating Figures of Church History
(Previously published by Baker Book House under the title
Ancient Portraits in Modern Frames, Vol. 2)

ISBN: 978-1-60374-638-0
eBook ISBN: 978-1-60374-687-8
Printed in the United States of America
© 1975, 2013 by Ardis A. Lockyer

Whitaker House
1030 Hunt Valley Circle
New Kensington, PA 15068
www.whitakerhouse.com

Library of Congress Cataloging-in-Publication Data (Pending)

1 2 3 4 5 6 7 8 9 10 11   **LU**   20 19 18 17 16 15 14 13

CONTENTS

"History is the essence of innumerable biographies."
—Thomas Carlyle

INTRODUCTION

CHURCH BIOGRAPHIES

Biographical reading and study is both fascinating and faithful, and church history is replete with the lives and deeds of saints—true knights—who fought under the banner of the Lord they loved. Many of them were men and women of action, as well as of vision. It mattered little to them where they pitched their tent, as long as they could serve Him to whom they owed so much. Stirring deeds and extraordinary accomplishments embroidered their lives and now kindle in our hearts the desire to emulate their faith, their sanctity, and their courage. Their imperishable record reminds us that we, too, can "make our lives sublime." Meditating upon the character and magnificent labors of great lives crowding the roll of church history, we are impressed with the fact of Christ as a living and working power in the life of man; and that what He did for and with them He can still accomplish through us. Robert Browning, in "One Word More," reminds us,

> Other heights in other lives, God willing:
> All the gifts from all the heights, your own, Love!

The biographies we have selected are of men who were outstanding and strategic witnesses for Christ in their own times, and who not only molded the thought and directed the action of the age in which they lived but who today, though dead, still speak.

At the burial of Caesar, Shakespeare makes Cassius say:

> The evil that men do lives after them,
> The good is oft interred with their bones.

While this sentiment is true of a great many who live without God, it is not applicable to the vast majority of church saints. Certainly they had their faults and made mistakes, for they were very human. But dominating their lives was the passion to serve God in a needy world, and, although hardy adventurers on the sea of life, buffeted and beset by violent storms, they came safely to port with rich cargoes. Their good was not interred with their bones. Their stories still thrill our hearts and create within us a desire to follow them as they followed God.

CHAPTER 1

MARTIN LUTHER: THE MONK WHO SHOOK THE WORLD

God had to shake the monk before that monk could shake the religious world of his day—and shake him He did! Much can be said in favor of the contention that Martin Luther, German of the Germans, was the greatest spiritual force in the world since the days of the apostle Paul. Thomas Carlyle could say of him, "Luther, too, is one of our spiritual heroes; a prophet to his own country and time." In the dark Middle Ages, a reformation was needed to throw off the tyranny of a powerful ecclesiastical yoke, but the Reformer had to be a product of his own times, with qualities that made him a citizen of the world and, in the wide sense, not for an age but for all time. Such a Reformer, as we will see, was Martin Luther.

All Christians who value their spiritual liberty should know of the life and labors of Luther. We owe our enjoyment of gospel privileges to the freedom he gained for the church from Rome's yoke. It pleased God to lead him through a spiritual experience so deep and abiding that an intense craving to know the Word of Truth was awakened in him, which resulted in his emancipation from religious bondage. God chose Luther to be the bringer of life to the darkened peoples of Europe and to blaze a trail of spiritual liberty for all time. But the conflict between the two opposing forces had first to be fought out in his own soul. Paul Lindemann, the prominent Lutheran pastor, says of Luther:

> It was the bold challenge of one man, flung out to the embattled forces of a despotic hierarchy, that four hundred years ago sounded the first note of human independence and broke the dread power that through the Dark Ages had kept the minds and the souls of men enthralled.... This year [1953] we are celebrating the four hundred and fiftieth anniversary of the man who set the wheels of Reformation progress going.

HIS BIRTH AND BOYHOOD

The whole world was shrouded in spiritual darkness when, on November 10, 1483, in the small town of Eisleben, Saxony, a son was born to Hans and Margaret Luther, their firstborn. Hans was a poor, ordinary mine laborer. One day, along with his wife, he went to the Winter Fair at Eisleben, and, during the tumult of one of the scenes, Frau Luther was taken with pains of travail and sought refuge in a house nearby, where she bore her child and called him Martin. Although the parents had very little of this world's goods, they were God-fearing in their way. Thomas Carlyle wrote of the importance of that lowly birth:

> In the whole world that day, there was not a more entirely unimportant-looking pair of people than this miner and his wife. And yet what were all the emperors, popes, and

potentates in comparison? There was born, once more, a mighty man whose light was to flame as a beacon over long centuries and epochs of the world, the whole world and its history were waiting for this man.

Carlyle then went on to say that Luther's lowly birth leads us back to another birth hour when One was born in the still meaner environment of a stable—One for whom Luther was to live and fight.

Born into a poor home and brought up poor, this child of poverty had to beg for bread, as the schoolchildren in those times did, singing door-to-door for alms and bread. Hardship was the poor boy's companion; no man and no thing would put on a false face to flatter Martin Luther. A boy of rude figure, yet with weak health, with his large, greedy soul full of all faculty and sensibility, he suffered greatly.

Hans gave his child the best education he could. Young Martin had a good intellect and was eager to learn and set himself to study law, but God had other plans for the son of poverty whose name was to become imperishable. It soon became evident that he had great natural advantages, all of which were to be harnessed to the chariot of the Lord. Luther was nineteen years of age when his companion Alexis was struck by lightning and fell dead at Luther's feet. Such a sudden blow smote his young heart, and he determined then and there to devote himself to God and to His service only. There developed within him a hunger for God, and he cried out with Job, "Oh, that I knew where I might find Him!" (See Job 23:3.)

HIS SPIRITUAL EXPERIENCES

In spite of his father's wishes, Martin entered an Augustine convent at Erfurt to train as a monk. Although to his parents this seemed the wrong step for their son to take, yet we can count it the first step in his spiritual development. To quote Carlyle again:

This was probably the first light-joint of the history of Luther, his purer will now first decisively uttering itself; but, for the moment it was still as one light-joint in an element of darkness. He says he was a pious monk: faithfully, painfully struggling to work out the truth of this high act of his: but it was to little purpose. His misery had not lessened: had rather, as it were, increased into infinitude.

Religious drudgeries, penances, and prayers could not relieve the burden of his soul. He lived in misery yet traveled far in his religious order, becoming a professor of philosophy at Wittenberg University and likewise its preacher. Strange to say, however, it was here that deliverance from darkness and despair and a burdensome life of fasts, prayers, and masses first came. At the time, the young monk was twenty-four years old, but he had never seen a Bible. The Word of God was precious in those days of no open vision. One day in the convent library, his eyes lighted upon an old copy of the Bible chained to the wall, and, poring over Paul's letter to the Romans, he read, *"The just shall live by faith"* (Romans 1:17; Hebrews 10:38; see also Habakkuk 2:4), and a new world opened to this searcher of truth. He came to love the Bible and determined to hold by it, as he did to the end. Perhaps the Scriptures have become too common. The world is now flooded with Bibles. If they were as scarce as in Luther's day, we might value them more.

The next event in Luther's pursuit of God came at Bologna. Crossing the Alps on a mission for the Catholic Church, he was entertained in a Benedictine convent. While there, he fell ill and was forced to remain for some time. Despair and darkness possessed him, and his soul was filled with remorse. The sense of his sinfulness troubled him, and the prospect of judgment filled him with dread. He had no inner peace. But when his terrors reached their highest pitch, the Pauline message he had discovered at Wittenburg forced itself upon him, and his spirit revived. Thus restored and comforted, he soon regained his health and resumed his journey.

This young German monk was twenty-seven years old when, in 1511, he saw Rome for the first time. Little did he know that his search for God would end here, and that his soul would find peace as the true church found a mighty Reformer. Because of the fierce conflict within, he came to the pope to obtain the indulgences he gave. All pilgrims had to climb the staircase known as *Scala Santa*, made up of twenty-eight marble steps in the Lateran Church, which ranked as the first Roman church in Christendom. The so-called Holy Staircase was said to have been brought from the palace of Pontius Pilate at Jerusalem to Rome in A.D. 326 by Empress Helena, mother of Constantine the Great. It received its name because it was said to be the staircase ascended by Jesus when He went up into the judgment hall—and stained by His blood when He came down again, wearing His mock crown.

This was an object of great veneration, and for centuries, its marble was worn down by the constant pilgrimages of the devout as they kissed the supposed blood spots of Christ. Martin Luther started to ascend this stair, crawling, to receive an indulgence for a thousand-year deliverance from the fire of purgatory once he reached the top of the staircase. He was shocked, however, by what he saw in Rome. When he was halfway up the stairs, he suddenly heard a voice like thunder saying, *"The just shall live by faith."* The message thrilled his soul, and he stood to his feet, overwhelmed. Luther said to himself, "This staircase can never be the ladder of salvation." At once, he became ashamed that he had become a victim of such a horrid superstition. The miracle had happened. The pursuit was ended. He had found God; or, should we say, God had found him. Shaking the dust off his feet, he fled Rome. He had left Wittenburg believing in justification by works; he returned believing in justification by faith.

Liberated from his religious shackles, Luther became the father of all true Protestants by protesting against the blasphemous abuses of the system of papal indulgences. When he nailed his "Ninety-five Theses" on the door of the Castel Church at Wittenburg, he little realized that "the blows of his hammer were to sound the death knell of an era of darkness and ring in an age of light." The miracle of what had happened to Luther at Rome is testified to by his son, Paul, named after the apostle through whose writings his father found salvation. In a glass case in the Library of Rudolstadt is a manuscript in the handwriting of Dr. Paul Luther, part of which reads,

> In the year 1544, my late dearest father, in the presence of us all, narrated the whole story of his journey to Rome. He acknowledged with great joy that, in that city, through the Spirit of Jesus Christ, he had come to the knowledge of the truth of the everlasting Gospel. It happened in this way. As he repeated his prayers on the Lateran staircase the words of the prophet Habakkuk came suddenly to his mind—*The just shall live by faith.* Thereafter, he ceased his prayers, returned to Wittenberg, and took this as the chief foundation of all his doctrine.

Luther's break with Rome and Catholic practices was radical. Evidence of his complete renunciation came when he cast off the vow of celibacy and married a nun, Catherine von Bora. He had always longed for domestic happiness, and, when no longer young, he found a wife as a practical testimony to his transformed life. Luther believed in burning his bridges behind him. His became a happy home, rich in love, even though it was simple. Sometimes his humor played with her little failings, but "his Kate" was inexpressibly dear to him. "Kate," he said to her one day, "you have a good husband who loves you. You are an empress. You are dearer than the kingdom of France and the dukedom of Venice."

Though affectionate, Luther was strict at home. Once, he would not allow his son to appear before him following some misdemeanor. This separation lasted three days and ended only when the lad wrote an apology and entreated forgiveness. When Luther's wife and others pleaded for leniency, Luther replied, "I would rather have a dead than an unworthy son." Perhaps the death of his little daughter Magdalene was the heaviest sorrow of his life. "My dear little daughter," he said as death parted them, "the spirit is willing but the flesh is weak."

The home was often filled with song. Luther called music "the grandest and sweetest gift of God." In the university garden at Wittenburg, the seat where Luther and his beloved wife would sit and give to the winds their fears with lute and song is pointed out to visitors. "Except theology," he would say, "there is no art which can be placed in comparison with music."

The home garden was a perpetual joy to this courageous man whose devout frame of mind enabled him to see God in flowers, birds, and animals. Like Francis of Assisi, he would talk winsomely to the birds. Speaking of flowers, he said, "If a man could make a single rose, we should give him an empire; yet roses and flowers no less beautiful are scattered in profusion over the world, and no one regards them." One day, watching the cattle in the field, he exclaimed, "There go the preachers, the bearers of milk, of butter, of cheese, and of wool, who daily preach faith in God and tell us to put our trust in Him, as our Father who cares for us and nourishes us." Such was the man who was to turn the religious world upside down and inside out.

HIS MARVELOUS ACCOMPLISHMENTS

Popular power became Luther's because of his love for humanity. Dollinger said of him, "His greatness of soul and his marvelous many-sidedness made him the man of his time and the man of his people. There were no conflicting impulses in his nature. He was a whole man, 'an absolute man; in him soul and body were not divided,' and thus the man through whom Europe was saved from Romish dominion, and the darkness of the Middle Ages scattered. Luther's salvation gave birth to Protestantism." His fight against the papacy was long and bitter, but he faced the conflict and challenge with heaven-given courage, and he emerged triumphant.

A Reformer

Luther's first challenge in the great task of Reformation came in October 1517, when Monk Tetzel falsely accused him of selling indulgences. Antagonism between these two monks deepened as Luther proved the falseness of Tetzel's statements by writing so strongly against Catholic practices. On December 10, 1520, the pope issued a bull forbidding Luther to continue in his protestations; but, amid a large crowd of people gathered at the Elster Gate at Wittenburg, he burned the bull. When he went out to meet the pope's legate at Augsburg, his fellow citizens who loved him watched him walk out to the gates, dressed in his brown monk's frock. They cried, "Luther forever!" But he replied, "Nay, Christ forever! All the wisdom of the world is childish foolishness compared with an acknowledgement of Christ."

At the Diet of Worms on April 17, 1521, a further test came when, before the assembled powers of the Roman Catholic world, he declared, "My conscience is bound by the Word of God. I cannot and will not recant....Were there as many devils in Worms as there are roof-tiles, I would go on." Later, he backed up this fearless declaration of independence with the public burning of man-made dicta of the Roman Catholic Church. Realizing the importance of his appearance at Worms, Luther had spent the previous night in prayer, asking that he might be guided aright. He knew that he would be facing the young emperor, Charles V, and many German princes, as well as papal authorities, when called upon to recant.

Many of his friends advised him with solemn entreaties not to appear before the diet, reminding him of the burning of another Reformer, John Huss; but no one and nothing could move him to desist, and he went forth to meet his foes. As Carlyle said, "The world's pomp and power sits there on this hand; on that stands up for God's truth one man, the poor miner Hans Luther's son." When commanded to recant, Luther replied, "Confute me by proofs of Scripture, or else by plain, just arguments: I cannot recant otherwise. For it is neither safe nor prudent to do aught against conscience. Here I stand: I can do no other: May God help me, amen!"

The emperor dismissed the gathering and deemed Luther a madman, one possessed by devils. Effective measures were taken to check the influence of his growing popularity and protestations. "Luther's appearance at that diet may be considered as the greatest scene in modern European history." In 1526 and 1529, there were two further diets, at Speier, when Rome tried again to curb this brave and defiant Reformer, who was becoming a growing menace to Catholic domination. But, at each diet, he defied threats, and, obeying his God-possessed conscience, he declared, "We are resolved, with the grace of God, to maintain the pure and exclusive preaching of His only Word, such as it is contained in the biblical books of the Old and New testaments, without adding anything thereto that may be contrary to it."

Thus, through the extraordinary intensity of his convictions, Luther saw the fires of Reformation spreading. There were no extravagances of fanaticism in him. Determined, he was yet sane. "For the great works of the Protestant Reformation which was to be served with voice and pen, a man of this caliber rather than a scholarly recluse was needed." Referring to the reforming principles of a previous Reformation preacher who never tired of inveighing against the intellectual density of the monks, a current saying had it, "Erasmus laid the egg but Luther hatched it"—and what a brood that hatching produced! All Protestant denominations owe their religious liberty to serve and worship God as His Word dictates to Luther's gallant defense of the saving truths of the gospel. What he taught about justification by faith and of the universal priesthood of all believers might well be called the Cornerstone of Protestantism.

The Reformer's influence still lives. The various branches of the Lutheran Church total up many millions of members. In America alone, there are well over three million adherents. "Lutheran" was a nickname given to the followers of Martin Luther by their enemies in the days of the Reformation. But, as Abdel R. Wenta expresses it, "*Lutheran* is a very inadequate name to give to a movement that is not limited to a person or an era but is as ecumenical and abiding as Christianity itself."

In his various protests, this fearless champion of truth revealed his love for picturesque and symbolic language. When he faced the king of England and the Roman hierarchy, his defense manifested how different he was from many other Reformers, in that he was essentially human, full of common sense, and likewise humorous. Hear him as he answers his foes: "Swine that you are! Burn me if you can and dare. Here I am; do your worst upon me. Scatter my ashes to all the winds—spread them through all the seas. My spirit shall pursue you still.…Luther shall leave you neither peace nor rest till he has crushed in your brows of brass and dashed out your iron brains."

Well, Luther was not burnt at the stake, nor were his ashes scattered; but his spirit lives on and pursues us still, calling us to stand up and be counted in these days of apostasy within the professed church, in which the courage to protect against everything alien to the Word of God is a scarce quality.

An Expositor

Natural gifts and spiritual power, coupled with a love for the Scriptures, made Luther the great biblical preacher and expositor his sermons and expositions reveal him to have been. Taught by God, he received clear insight into fundamental truths. He believed in studying the sacred Word itself. "Through so many commentaries and books, the dear Bible is buried, so that people do not look at the text itself. It is far better to see with our own eyes than with other people's eyes." Another saying of Luther's was this: "A layman who has the Scriptures is more to be trusted than pope or council without it." While he was a young professor at Wittenburg, he commenced to expound the Word by lecturing on the Psalms. He had a hunger for the Scriptures as one who had been long deprived of necessary food. In his *History of Christian Preaching*, Professor Harwood Pattison says,

> Luther's choice of words was fresh and natural; he had at his command fancy, imagination, irony, sarcasm. The anecdote was always ready, the allegory revealed its hidden meaning as he used it, and he was a master of the plain speech needed for popular exposition.

The people who heard Luther preach and teach said that his words were "half battles." Philipp Melanchthon, his close friend in his trials and triumphs, said that the secret of Luther's effectiveness was that "his words were born not on his lips but in his soul." From the heart he spoke to the heart and thus moved audiences. Fearless plainness characterizes many of his utterances. Heinrich Heine, drawing attention to this feature of Luther's preaching, said, "The fine discernment of Erasmus, and the gentleness of Melanchthon, had never done so much for us as the divine brutality of Brother Martin." Robert Browning wrote of him as "grand rough old Martin Luther."

As an expositor and translator of Scripture, he stands without a peer in his familiarity with the spiritual meaning of the Word of God. After three months of incessant and enthusiastic labor, he completed his marvelous translation of the New Testament. When he had finished translating the whole Bible from Latin into the language of his own nation, he wrote, "You have now the Bible in German. Now I will cease from my labors. You have now what you want. Only see to it and use it after my death. It has cost me labor enough. What an unspeakable grace it is that God speaks to us." Today, multitudes have the Bible in the clearest and purest English possible. The question is, do they read it as passionately as Luther did?

As an author, Luther left the church some masterly works. His *Longer and Shorter Catechisms*, written in 1529, contain many of his pungent sayings. His *Commentary on Romans* remains to this day. Godet called it the "Cathedral of Christian Faith." The reading of the preface of Luther's *Romans* commentary led to John Wesley's heart being "strangely warmed" and, later, to his mighty revival ministry. His *Commentary on Galatians* is a masterpiece. Galatians was Luther's favorite book of the Bible because it unfolds the Protestant doctrine he thrust upon the world, namely, justification by faith. He regarded Galatians as his spouse among Bible books and named it after his beloved wife. "My own Epistle," he called it, "to what I have plighted my troth. It is my Katie von Bora." He found in Galatians a source of strength for his own faith and life and an armory of weapons for his reforming work.

Among the evangelical themes and doctrines Luther loved to preach and write about, outstanding ones can be mentioned.

First and foremost was justification by faith, which he so expertly expounds in his work on Galatians. Of such a doctrinal truth, he wrote, "In my heart this article reigns alone, and shall reign, namely, faith in my dear Lord Christ, who is the only Beginning, Middle, and End of all my spiritual and divine thoughts. In His death He is a Sacrifice, satisfying for our sins. In His resurrection, the Conqueror. In His ascension, the King. In His intercession, the High Priest."

Second, there was the forgiveness of sins, which he preached and taught with great power and effect. To one concerned about

God's direct forgiveness, Luther wrote, "It is God's command that we should believe our own sins are forgiven. Hear what Saint Bernard says: 'The testimony of the Holy Spirit in thy heart is this—Thy sins are forgiven thee.'" There can be no question about what he meant when he used this descriptive illustration: "A man's heart is like some foul stable; wheelbarrows and shovels are of little use except to remove some of the surface filth, and to litter all the passages in the process. What is to be done with it? Turn the Elbe into it. The flood will sweep away the pollution."

There is the well-known story about Luther's encounter with the devil, who confronted him with a list of his sins. Luther threw the ink bottle at the devil, telling him to write over the sins, "The blood of Jesus Christ cleanseth from all sins." This story bristles with the Reformer's personal assurance of sins forgiven. How we need in the pulpits of today a revival of Martin Luther's sturdy straightforwardness in the preaching of the saving truths of the gospel.

HIS CLOSING DAYS

Samuel Johnson reminded us that "it matters not how a man dies, but how he lives." Yet how a man lives often determines how he dies. Does not the Bible say, "Mark the perfect man—his end is peace"? (See Psalm 37:37.) Martin Luther had an old body before he was sixty years of age. Because of his diseased frame, he became irritable and a trial to his friends. Writing to Zwingli, a fellow Reformer, he described himself as "a worn-out, lazy, tired, old, and now one-eyed man." But he remained active to the end. On Wednesday, February 17, 1546, those around him noticed how feeble and ailing he was. During the afternoon and evening, he complained about a pain in his chest, yet he was cheerful. His two sons, Paul and Hans—thirteen and fourteen years old, respectively—sat up all night with their father. Early in the morning, he awoke with sweat on his brow and said to his boys, "It is the cold sweat of death. I must yield up my spirit, for my sickness increaseth." Medicine was given him, and then he repeated three times, "Father, into Thy hands I commend my spirit. Thou hast redeemed me, Thou faithful God. Truly God has so loved the world."

His sorrowful young sons said to him, "Venerable Father, do you die trusting in Christ, and in the doctrine you have constantly preached?" Luther answered a joyous yes—his last word on earth—as he folded his hands on his breast, and at 4:00 a.m., February 18, 1546, he was not, for God took the warrior home to his rest and reward. What better tribute can we pay to such a mighty Reformer than the one expressed by Carlyle in *Heroes and Hero Worship?*:

> I will call this Luther a true great man: great in intellect: in courage, affection and integrity: one of our most lovable and precious men....A right spiritual Hero and Prophet: once more, a true Son of Nature, a fact for whom these centuries and many that are to come yet, will be thankful to Heaven.

In his most valuable work, *Laws for Common Life*, Dr. R. W. Dale has this most appealing summary of Martin Luther's wonderful life and labors:

> He had a fiery and passionate hatred of falsehood and of sin; a dauntless courage in the assertion of the claims of truth and righteousness. He had a boundless faith and a boundless joy in God. His joy was of a masculine kind, and made him stronger for his work. His faith was of a masculine kind, and relieved him from worrying doubts and fears about his soul's affairs. He had his gloomy times, his conflicts with principalities and powers in dismal and solitary places; but he had no morbid dreams about the sanctity of misery, nor did he suppose that the ever-blessed God finds any satisfaction in the self-inflicted sufferings of

his children. His massive face and robust form were the outward and visible signs of the vigour and massiveness of his moral and religious character. He was a man, and did not try to be anything else. God made him a man; what was he that he should quarrel with God's work? He had flesh and blood; he could not help it. He did not desire to help it. He ate heartily, and enjoyed seeing his friends at dinner. He married a wife and loved her; and he loved God none the less. He liked music and songs as well as preaching and sermons. He could laugh as well as preach. He had a genial humour as well as deep devoutness. He was a brave man, strong and resolute, with abounding life of all kinds; a saint of a type with which for many evil centuries Christendom had been unfamiliar.

Around the time of Martin Luther's birth, many Protestant churches commemorate his great work by a Reformation Day, when his courageous challenge of the embattled forces of a despotic religious hierarchy are reemphasized from pulpit and platform. American churches, in particular, recognize such a day, and rightly so, seeing that the righteous principles for which he so nobly fought are woven into the very Constitution of the United States. The religious freedom so characteristic of the New World is the fruit of the Reformation. As Paul Lindemann states it:

The spirit of Luther influenced the framers of that historic document in Philadelphia. Without him, the statement never could have been written that all men are created equal. Never could the principle have been adopted among a whole nation that there must be freedom of the individual, of speech, of press, of conscience. Luther's principle is echoed in the words of the first amendment to the Constitution—Congress shall make no law respecting an establishment of religion or prohibiting the free exercise thereof. We owe the blessed institutions of this land of the free to Martin Luther....As the result of the Reformation, we have today a marvelous system of education of which we may truthfully call Luther the founder.

Reformation Day gives preachers the opportunity to declare the truths that delivered the German monk from the shackles of sin and of religious oppression. The verse that gripped his heart and led him from a religion of fear to one of faith was the four-time-repeated one: *"The just shall live by faith."* This oft-quoted verse had a mysterious influence on the life of Luther. It was a creative sentence, both for the Reformer and the reformed. Whenever this evangelical verse is preached on, Luther's tribute to its revolutionary power in his own life should be quoted:

> Before those words broke upon my mind, I hated God and was angry with Him because, not content with frightening us sinners by the Law, and the miseries of life, He still further increased our torture by the Gospel. But when, by the Spirit of God, I understood these words—*"The just shall live by faith"*—then I felt born again like a new man: I entered through the open door into the very Paradise of God....In very truth, this text was to me the true gate of Paradise.

Salvation and justification by faith thereafter became Luther's predominant theme and the foundation of his undying work of Reformation. Here are some of his gems as to the substance and efficacy of saving faith:

+ Faith and human understanding are one against another.
+ Faith depends upon the Word.
+ Faith is a Christian's treasure.
+ Faith in Christ destroys sin.
+ Faith makes us Christ's heritage.

+ Faith is to build certainty on God's mercy.

+ To doubt is sin and everlasting death.

All of us are familiar with Luther's famous, stirring Reformation hymn, with its ringing confidence in God:

> Did we in our own strength confide,
> Our striving would be losing,
> Were not the right Man on our side,
> The Man of God's own choosing.
> Dost ask who that may be?
> Christ Jesus, it is He;
> Lord Sabaoth His name,
> From age to age the same,
> And He must win the battle.[1]

---

1. Martin Luther, "A Mighty Fortress Is Our God," 1529.

CHAPTER 2

GEORGE WISHART:
THE NOBLE AND ILLUSTRIOUS
SCOTTISH MARTYR

There can be no better approach to a study of Scottish martyrology than through the gateway of the Protestant Reformation that Martin Luther was so conspicuously identified with. The great principles that actuated the Reformation leaders in Europe became the central contendings and abiding heritage of Scottish Covenanters and martyrs, who, like many earlier Reformers, sealed their testimony with their blood. Scotland is preeminently the land of those who were willing to die for the faith. The writing on an old stone in Kirkintilloch, erected in 1685 to commemorate two Scots worthies who died for Christ, reads,

'Twas Martyrs' Blood Brought Scotland's Liberty.

The thousands who stained the moors and glens with their blood are numbered among those slain for the Word of God, whose souls are under the altar, waiting for the Judge to avenge their blood. (See Revelation 6:9.)

The standard biography and classic on the subject of the Scottish Covenant is the astonishing work of a lowly, self-taught peasant who lived on the moors far from the haunts of man, namely, John Howie, author of *The Scots Worthies*. This historic volume, appearing in 1775, is made up of stories the author received from those who had passed through the fire. Howie is all aglow with the glory of covenanting days in Scotland, and he expresses concern over Scotland selling its dearly bought religious freedom for a mess of pottage. The author exclaims,

> What would be the conception of these courses of defection of our Reformers and later Martyrs, if they were given a short furlough from their scenes of glory, to take a short view of their apostacizing children: for if innocent Hamilton, godly and patient Wishart, apostolic Knox, eloquent Rollock, worthy Davidson, courageous Melville, prophetic Welsh, majestic Bruce, great Henderson, renowned Gillespie, learned Binning, pious Gray, laborious Durham, heavenly-minded Rutherford, the faithful Guthries, diligent Blair, heart-melting Livingstone, religious Wellwood, orthodox and practical Brown, zealous and stedfast Cameron, honest-hearted Cargill, sympathising McWard, persevering Blackader, the evangelical Traills, constant and pious Renwick, etc., were filed off from the Assembly of the First-Born, and but as Commissioners to haste down from the ascent of God to behold how quickly their offspring are gone out of the way, piping and dancing after a golden calf, ah! With what vehemency would their spirits be affected, to see their labourious structure almost razed to the foundations, by those to whom they committed the custody of their great Lord's patience.

Howie ends this roll call of heroes, and their reaction to defection from the faith they died to preserve, by quoting old Samuel Rutherford's letter to the Earl of Cassillis:

> Your honourable ancestors, with the hazard of their lives, brought Christ into our lands, and it shall be cruelty to posterity if ye lose Him to them.

If that was the religious condition in Scotland in Howie's time, where are we now, over two hundred years later? We say that "the blood of the martyrs is the seed of the church," but the impotent, divided church of today knows little of the martyr spirit and faith. Scottish martyrs, over eighteen thousand of them, have their names engraved in stone in Edinburgh, which is called by way of preeminence "The Martyrs' Memorial." The history of many of those and others can be traced in Foxe's *Book of Martyrs*, which, although it makes for sobering reading, is a tonic for faith. But what better Book of Martyrs is there than the Bible itself, as Hebrews 11 proves?

> They climbed the steep ascent to heaven
> Through peril, toil, and pain.
> O God, to us may grace be given,
> To follow in their train!

Some have suggested that we no longer "follow in their train," or emulate their sacrificial spirit, but prefer to follow more comfortably *in* a train. Well, let us think of one who did climb the steep ascent to heaven—"the godly and patient" George Wishart, as John Howie described him, who was among the first in Scotland to be martyred. A memorial to him stands in Fordum Churchyard, about two miles from where he was born, and bears this inscription:

> This Monument is erected to the Memory of
> Scotland's First and Most Illustrious Martyr,
> George Wishart.

We do not have as much rich biographical material for study as in the case of John Knox, for Wishart's full life story was not written. Yet he fills a niche all his own in the great annals of Scottish history and is portrayed in a fourfold way.

1. AS A GENTLEMAN

Foxe called this renowned Dundee preacher "George Wishart—Gentleman." He was believed to be the only son of James Wishart, of Pitarrow, Kincardinshire. The date of his birth is uncertain but is said to be between 1513 and 1514, in Mansion House, Pitarrow, long ago destroyed. The Wisharts were an ancient and honorable family, aristocratic and well-connected. George's father was of French descent, but his mother came from Fife, Scotland. A writer of the time described him as "a son of Pitarrow, the worthiest person of all who supported the new doctrines in the Kingdom." James Melville, another renowned Covenanter, wrote in his diary, "The maist godlie, learned, and noble Scots Martyr, George Wishart." Sir Walter Scott said of him, "This martyr to the cause of the Reformation was a man of honourable birth, great wisdom and eloquence, and of primitive piety."

The Bible reminds us that *"not many wise,…not many noble are called"* (1 Corinthians 1:26); but thank God some are—among them George Wishart, God's gentleman, who will ever remain a witness to those in the ranks of nobility who, because of their culture, education, and possessions, could be a great asset to the cause of Christ, if only the Scottish martyr's faith and surrender were theirs.

2. AS A SCHOLAR

In respect to his early days, little is known of George Wishart's history and education. Such facts as we do have are related to his later years. We have reliable information that he was employed as a teacher in a school in Montrose, the first town in Scotland to teach Greek. Wishart taught German, which was counted as heresy by the Roman Catholic Church. In 1538, he was summoned by Bishop Hepburn on a charge of heresy for teaching German, and, threatened with a prosecution for teaching the German New Testament without authority, he was compelled to retreat to England. He was excommunicated by the bishop of Brechin with the accusation, "Thou false heretic, renegade, traitor, thief, and deceiver of the people, thou despisest the Holy Church, and in like case condemnest my Lord Governor's authority. Therefore curse thee, deliver thee into the devil's hands and give thee, in commandment, that thou preach no more."

In 1540, Wishart left England for Germany, where he remained for two or three years and was associated with the Swiss Reformation. Being impressed with the Swiss Confession, he translated it from Latin into his own tongue. Returning to England, he took up residence at Cambridge, where the nucleus of the English Reformation was to be found. He enrolled as a member of Corpus Christi College, intending to study and teach, and remained there about two years. Little is known about this period, however. We can assume that, with his thirst for knowledge, his stay in such a collegiate town proved to be a great spiritual and mental stimulus.

3. AS A PREACHER

As Wishart had embraced the principles of the Protestant faith, these formed the absorbing themes of his preaching, and he became eloquent in their declaration. He labored for a while at the Church of Saint Nicolas, Bristol, where his messages were clear and decisive. "God's way of life for sinners is through faith in the work of Jesus Christ" was the key theme of his preaching. To the delight of John Knox, he preached Luther's doctrine wherever he went. "None but Christ—Christ as Mediator, Lawgiver, Example, Friend—such was the gospel which George Wishart preached."

He returned to Montrose, not to teach but to preach the everlasting gospel. Having commenced his work there, he was happy to go back. He rented a house a few doors away from the Roman Catholic Church and exercised a most effective ministry there. Preaching was a lost art in Scotland in those days, and thus many gathered to hear him proclaim the gospel. From Montrose, Wishart went to Dundee, which had the honor of being the first burgh in Scotland to openly embrace the Reformation. Because of its ardent zeal for the Reformed cause, it became known as "The Scotch Geneva" or "The Second Geneva." One day, Dr. Alexander Whyte, of Edinburgh, asked his Bible class, "Why was Dundee called 'The Scotch Geneva' after Wishart's day?" Two answers were given as to why the city had been raised to such a primary position: first, the early labors of Wishart himself, because Dundee was one of his chief resorts and spheres of ministry. Here he preached publicly with great profit, lecturing at one time on Romans "to the great admiration of all who heard him."

The second reason was because of the influence of those who imbibed his spirit and followed up his labors. For many years, a Wishart Memorial Church has flourished there. The ever-increasing spread of Reformation truth had to be stopped, and Cardinal Beaton ordered Wishart to leave the city. Sorrowfully, he obeyed. Driven out by priestly devices, he said, "I have offered unto you the word of salvation and with hazard of my life. I have remained among you. Now ye yourselves refuse me and, therefore, I must leave my innocence to be declared by my God."

This noble defender of the faith went eastward and, following the way of his royal Master, was persecuted as he fled from one city to another. Ultimately, he came to Ayrshire, where he was welcomed by those hailing the dawn of the Reformation. In Ayr, where he began his labor, he preached with great power and freedom to the faithful. Rome, however, was determined to silence this fearless preacher of the gospel. The Archbishop of Glasgow came to Ayr to compel Wishart to desist, but to no avail. Forced to leave Ayr, Wishart went on to Galston to preach, but he was forbidden to do so by the sheriff. He went out into the fields, saying, "Christ Jesus is as mighty in the fields as in the church. And I find that He Himself preached oftener in the desert, at the seaside, and other places judged profane than in the temple at Jerusalem." The people came in great numbers to hear him in the open air. One day he preached for three hours, with far-reaching results. Lawrence Rankine, Laird of Schaw, one of the most wicked men in the countryside, was melted to tears and converted to God.

After a month in Ayrshire, hearing of the desolation in Dundee because of famine and pestilence, Wishart returned to the historic city and received a joyful welcome by a faithful band. The spot where he chose to preach in Cowgate became known as Wishart's Arch. Here he stood or sat, inspecting and helping the sick, and preaching a message of comfort to the needy. He took as his text *"He sent his word, and healed them"* (Psalm 107:20), the verse which was embodied in the inscription on the arch.

> During the plague of 1544, George Wishart preached from the parapet of this port, the people standing within the gate, and the plague-stricken lying without in booths. *"He sent his word, and healed them"* (Psalm 107:20).

During this terrible period, Wishart was diligent in visiting and comforting those in extremity, not only preaching to them but also feeding them with necessary food. "The preacher pointed all the sick and dying, not to shrine or image of St. Rogue, the patron saint of plague-stricken folk, but to Jesus Christ, the Great Physician and Healer of both soul and body, and thus raised all the hearts of those who heard him."

Laboring as I did in Dundee for many years, it was always an inspiration to visit Wishart's Arch and bless God for his battle for spiritual liberty.

But, while Wishart was doing good, the devil sought to do him harm. Cardinal Beaton attempted to assassinate this friend of the disconsolate by bribing a corrupted priest, a most desperate character, to slay him. One day, as Wishart ended his sermon, the priest stood at the foot of the pulpit with a drawn dagger beneath his loose gown. But Wishart's sharp eye detected danger, and he said to the priest, "My friend, what would you do?" The priest reached for the dagger to slay Wishart, but he was not quick enough, for Wishart grabbed it. The priest fell down and confessed his sin. The congregation cried, "Deliver the traitor to us, or else we will take him by force." Christlike, Wishart protected the repentant priest and saved his life.

Once the plague abated, Wishart left Dundee, saying, "The battle here is over, and God calls me to another." Invitations to preach came from many places, but he went to Montrose for a time of rest and meditation. The malice of Cardinal Beaton followed him, however, and another snare was set to destroy him, but God delivered him. When refreshed, he went on to Leith, where he met many saints who desired to hear him preach. Wishart said to them, "Dare ye and others hear, then let my God provide for me as best pleaseth Him." The next Sabbath, he preached to a large, responsive audience. Going on to East Lothian, he visited several churches in which gentry and common people alike gathered to hear his outspoken messages against the papacy. In his messages, he foretold of the shortness of his time, for he instinctively felt that he was approaching the day of his death—Rome's pressure was increasing: "What differ I from a dead man, except that I eat and drink? So this time God hath used my labours to the instruction of others, and to the disclosing of darkness: now, I lurk as a man that was ashamed, and dursn't show myself before men."

At Haddington, where he went from East Lothian, Wishart met John Knox, who became one of his most attentive hearers, and waited upon him. Knox's experience of saving grace can be traced to Wishart's influence. But Wishart received a letter that troubled him. It was in the form of a refusal to let him preach in the town. Rebuking those who barred him from preaching, he said, "O Lord, how long shall it be that Thy Holy Word shall be despised, and men shall not regard their salvation? Fearful shall be the plagues that shall ensue for this contempt. With fire and sword shalt thou be plagued, even thou, Haddington, especially." For an hour-and-a-half, he delivered his soul after this fashion. He had become disheartened over the decline of the Reformed cause, and he spoke to John Knox about his weariness and of the shadow of approaching doom.

4. AS A MARTYR

Wishart was forced to leave Haddington, and John Knox was eager to accompany and defend him. But Wishart forbade him, saying, "One is sufficient for our sacrifice." The two like-minded hearts embraced affectionately, and then Wishart departed. He came to Ormiston House to stay the night, and after worship he retired to rest. At midnight, however, the house was surrounded, and he sensed what would happen. The demand came for Earl Bothwell to open the gate. George Wishart said to him, "Open the gates; the blessed will of my God be done."

He was taken prisoner, brought to Edinburgh, and then taken to the Sea Tower in Saint Andrews, where he was imprisoned in the "Bottle Dungeon." He remained there from January through March 1546. He suffered greatly during these months, yet he wrote much, all of which his foes suppressed. Word came that he was to appear to answer a charge of sedition and heresy. He came before Cardinal Beaton and made a bold defense. As he entered the church for his trial, Wishart passed a poor man begging for alms, and he gave him his purse. The accusation was read by John Lauder, a priest, who then asked, "What answereth thou to these things, thou renegade, traitor, thief, which we have proved against thee?"

George Wishart bowed his knees and looked to God for an answer. Then, he gave three reasons why he should not be condemned. The verdict, however, was "Guilty," and he was sentenced to die the next day. It is said that he prayed, "O immortal God! How long shalt Thou suffer the great cruelty of the ungodly to exercise their fury upon Thy servants which do further Thy Word in this world?" On the morning of the scheduled execution, he breakfasted with the captain of the castle and a few others. He discussed with them the Lord's suffering and death, and then he dispensed the Lord's Supper for the first time, according to the Protestant form in Scotland.

The fire was made ready, and gunners stood by, prepared to shoot if any escape was attempted. Wishart's hands were bound behind his back with an iron chain to the middle of his waist. As he was being led to the stake, he met beggars pleading for money, but the doomed saint said, "I want my hands wherewith I was wont to give you, but the merciful Lord vouchsafe you necessaries for your bodies and souls." Reaching the stake, he kneeled and prayed three times, "O Thou Savior of the world, have mercy upon me. Father of heaven, I commend my spirit into Thy hands!" Then he addressed the sympathetic people gathered to see him burned, saying, "I beseech you, Christian brethren and sisters, be not offended at the Word of God for the torments and afflictions which ye see prepared for me....For this cause was I sent, that I should suffer fire for Christ's sake. Consider and behold my visage. Ye shall not see me change my color. This grim fire I fear not, and so I pray you to do, if persecution come unto you....I know surely that my soul shall sup with my Savior this night, ere it be six hours, for whom I suffer this."

Then he prayed for his accusers, "I forgive them with all my heart: I beseech Christ to forgive them," thereby emulating the example of the Master. He forgave his executioner, who asked, "Sir, I pray you, forgive me, for I am not guilty of your death." Wishart replied, "Come hither to me," and, kissing him, he said, "Lo! Here is a token that I forgive thee. My heart, do thine office." Believing that persecution turns its votaries into victims, Wishart said of Cardinal Beaton, who never rested until he saw the Reformer die, "He who from yonder place beholdeth me with such pride shall within a few days lie in the same, as ignominiously as he is now seen proudly to rest in himself."

The trumpet sounded, and Wishart was hanged on a gibbet and then burned. As the historian describes the scene, "The pile was fired, the powder exploded, the flames arose, and Wishart was dismissed by a painful death to blessed immortality in the next world." George Wishart was only thirty-one years of age when he was slain on March 1, 1546, for "the Word of God and the testimony of Jesus," and the trumpets sounded for him on the other side. "Many cruelties were exercised," says the historian Scott, "but that which excited public feeling to the highest degree was the barbarous death of George Wishart, whose burning dates the new birth of the Scottish Church and of the Scottish Nation." His cruel death caused great mourning. The people were indignant, feeling that an innocent lamb had been slain.

But although God buries His workmen, He carries on His work, and the effect of Wishart's martyrdom was to give impetus to the Reformation cause and doctrines. As we shall see, John Knox, the spiritual son of Wishart, proved to be a most worthy successor. For ourselves, the lessons to be learned from the labors of the renowned Covenanters are obvious.

First, we should value our spiritual heritage and make the most of our religious liberty. There are three kinds of liberty to preserve: (1) *civil* liberty, such as Bruce, Wallace, and Cromwell fought for; (2) *religious* liberty, procured by Knox, Wishart, the Covenanters, as well as by the Pilgrim Fathers; and (3) *spiritual* liberty, which the Savior secured for us by the shedding of His blood. In the law of recurrence, history repeats itself, and religious liberty is becoming scarcer through the spread of atheistic Communism and the continuing domination of Catholicism.

Second, we must possess the courage of God in the face of opposition. George Wishart never flinched, nor did he change the color of his countenance, as he was burned at the stake. Threats, dungeons, and fires could not frighten this valiant soul. Alas, there are multitudes today who are cowards. They do not have the courage of conviction. They are afraid to commit themselves to Christ and confess Him before the world, and too often they fill a coward's grave. God is calling today for spiritual heroes. May we be found among the number willing to be faithful even unto death!

Third, we see the victory of grace in that Wishart never retaliated, as his attitude at the stake reveals. He died, as his Savior did, forgiving his enemies and praying for their salvation. If Wishart's death meant Scotland's new birth, the outcome of Christ's martyrdom is our regeneration. The executioner said to Wishart that he was "not guilty of [his] death," but we were guilty of the crucifixion of the Lord of Glory, for it was our sins that nailed Him to the cross. The martyr kissed the man putting him to death, and for us there is also the kiss of forgiveness and reconciliation, "Kiss the Son!"

The Son of God goes forth to war, a kingly crown to gain;
His blood-red banner streams afar:
Who follows in His train?
Who now can drink His cup of woe,
triumphant over pain,
Who patient bears His cross below,
He follows in His train.[2]

---

2. Reginald Heber, "The Son of God Goes Forth to War," 1827.

CHAPTER 3

JOHN KNOX:
THE FEARLESS PREACHER WHO
REBUKED A QUEEN

It is fitting that the compelling portrait of the indomitable and fearless John Knox should hang next to the picture of the sweetest and saintliest Reformer, George Wishart, in God's portrait gallery of saints. With the latter's martyrdom, his mantle fell upon Knox, and he became a prominent figure in the troubled life of Scotland. He gladly would have shared the fate of his teacher and friend, and although he was not to die a martyr, the iron went into his soul, as well, and for many years he lived the life of an exile and a wanderer for conscience's sake.

Carlyle tells us, "One comfort is that great men, taken up in any way, are profitable company. We cannot look, however imperfectly, upon a great man without gaining something by him. He is the living light-fountain which it is good and pleasant to be near."

This is especially true of John Knox, whose company is always profitable. Much can be gained from learning about his life and labors. In the best sense, it was always "good and pleasant to be near" him. Recognizing Knox as the most conspicuous figure on the pages of Scottish history, Carlyle says in *Hero a Priest*, "In the history of Scotland, I can find but one epoch: we may say it contains nothing of world-interest but this Reformation by Knox."

A MAN OF CULTURE

There is a division of opinion about the time and place of Knox's birth. The general opinion is that he was born around 1505, in Haddington, Scotland, the son of a small landowner, and that he was educated at the grammar school in Haddington, proceeding to Glasgow University when he was about seventeen years of age. There is no mention of him taking any degrees, nor does he appear to have made a mark as a scholar during the years of his education. He was ordained to the priesthood when he was twenty-five and became a professor of logic and a tutor in the family of Hugh Douglas of East Lothian. Facts about his early years are scanty, for he lived for many years in near obscurity. Apparently, he adhered to the Catholic doctrines in which he had been educated, and he was thus well qualified to combat them, as he fearlessly did after he embraced the doctrines of the Reformation, having heard them preached by Reformers like Patrick Hamilton and George Wishart.

Around 1544, Knox openly declared himself to be a Protestant, and in 1547, he was called to officiate as the Protestant minister of Saint Andrews, Scotland, where he had fled from the persecution against Reformers that was raging at the time. But his ministry there lasted only a few months. Saint Andrews was attacked by the French fleet. The city capitulated, and Knox, with other refugees, was condemned for nineteen months to work at the galleys—hard and cruel labor that injured Knox's health for life. After his release in 1549, he returned to Scotland, but, finding little to do there, he took refuge in Berwick and then afterward in Newcastle. During his stay in England, he met and married the daughter of a landed gentleman of Northumberland. In 1555, he and his wife went to Dieppe, and then to Geneva, where he visited John Calvin and was greatly influenced by his teachings. After his return to Scotland, he became the most representative preacher of Calvinism. "Scotland is the triumph of Calvinism, and to John Knox in its first victorious stages that triumph is mainly due."

He possessed a high mental caliber and wonderful eloquence, and his fame as a preacher spread far and wide. He was made chaplain to King Edward VI in 1551 and was afterward offered the bishopric of Rochester, which he refused, finding it contrary to his principles. In 1559, he returned to Scotland, where the fires of persecution were abating but had not been quenched. It was a critical time, for several Protestant preachers were on the point of being tried for their lives, and Knox, who had been condemned in early days of the persecution, was again proclaimed a heretic.

The queen-regent was alarmed over the sympathy felt by the common people for these ministers who were to be tried, and their trial was abandoned. Knox was appointed minister of the historic Church of Saint Giles, Edinburgh, in 1560, and he stayed there during the remaining twelve years of his life, delivering messages week by week that brought salvation to many. In addition to his potent pulpit labors, he furthered the cause of Christ with his numerous trenchant writings. He published works against the worship of Mary and the Catholic Church. Perhaps his greatest work, published after his death, is *The History of Reformation in Scotland*, which gives us a mirror of the writer himself and of his times.

Knox's influence became far-reaching, even to being recognized as the great ecclesiastical power of his country. Intelligence and moral and spiritual power enabled him to sway the common and cultured classes alike. A religious giant of a man, he was also intensely patriotic. Devotion to Christ ennobled his character and made him God's battle-ax and weapon of war. To quote Carlyle's appreciation of his noble life,

> That he could rebuke Queens, and had such weight among those proud turbulent Nobles, proud enough whatever else they were: and could maintain to the end a kind of virtual Presidency and Sovereignty in that wild realm he who was only "a subject born with the same"—this of itself will prove to me that he was found close at hand to be no mean acrid man, but at heart a healthful, strong, sagacious man.

A MAN OF CHRIST

It is not easy to determine exactly when Knox gained an interest in the Savior's blood and his chains of Catholicism fell off, or when his heart was freed to rise, go forth, and follow the Savior. It would seem that several factors contributed to his surrender to divine claims, making him God's hero of the Scottish Reformation.

First of all, there was his association with George Wishart. The time he spent with this godly martyr was possibly the greatest formative influence in Knox's life. We do not meet him in Scottish history until after the death of Wishart, yet he was his close companion, standing by him and carrying a sword, ready to defend Wishart while he preached. His powerful preaching deepened Knox's religious impression and strengthened his hatred for the Roman Church. Knox was ever eager to assist Wishart. One night, he saw him taken prisoner and committed to the dungeon. How eager he was to accompany him. But Wishart forbade his zealous disciple. Taking his sword from him, he said, "Nay, return to your bairns, and God bless you! One is sufficient for sacrifice." If Knox witnessed Wishart's calm and courageous death at the stake, it must have had a profound effect upon his life.

Second, the words Knox uttered as he came to die indicate the probable means of his conversion. To his wife, he expressed his dying wish: "Go and read where I cast my first anchor." She read the seventeenth chapter of John and a part of Calvin's *Commentary on the Ephesians*. After witnessing the cruel martyrdom of Wishart, Knox may have gone home and read the high priestly prayer of Jesus, which he found so applicable, and the miracle happened, and he became one of those given to Christ by His Father. As Stephen's heroic martyrdom doubtless had a share in the transformation of Saul of Tarsus, so the blood of Wishart the martyr became a seed in Knox the Reformer.

Third, there was the confession of his faith in Christ as Savior. God gave John Knox a deep insight into the truth. His understanding of the inner meaning of the redemptive work of Christ is borne out by this paragraph from one of his sermons:

> There is no other name by which men can be saved but that of Jesus, and that all reliance on the merits of others is vain and delusive: that the Saviour having by his own sacrifice sanctified and reconciled to God those who should inherit the promised kingdom, all other sacrifices which men pretend to offer for sin are blasphemous—all ought to hate sin which is so odious before God that no sacrifice but the death of His Son could satisfy it.

Such evangelical preaching raised the ire of the papal authorities to the extent that they passed the sentence of death upon Knox, but he went into hiding. Instead, the papists made an effigy of him and burnt it.

Fourth, there was his prevailing intercession. Knox could not have been the mighty man of prayer he was had there not been the foundation of salvation. The spiritual emancipation from Rome of his beloved native land was always on his heart and in his prayers. One day, burdened about the very many still in darkness, he cried,

"O God, give me Scotland or I die!" God gave him Scotland, and the land has never lost the impact of his heart cries. The queen of the country said that she feared the prayers of John Knox more than an army of soldiers. Does Satan tremble when he sees us on our knees?

A MAN OF CHASTISEMENT

From the time of his association with George Wishart, Knox was a marked man. He had good reason to fear that he would be the next to be taken and sacrificed as a martyr. He took a bold step and made himself more conspicuous when he accepted, albeit with reluctance, the call to minister to a small body of Reformers at Saint Andrews. When the city fell to the French, Knox was taken captive and made to toil wearily at the oars. As the ship passed the Scottish coast on the way to France, one of the prisoners pointed out to him the steeple of the church in which he had ministered. "Ah, I see the steeple of that place where God first in public opened my mouth to His glory," said the emaciated prisoner, "and I am fully persuaded, how weak soever I now appear, that I shall not depart this life till that my tongue shall glorify His godly name in the same place."

Those nineteen months as a galley slave took their toll on his health, and he was never the same afterward. Returning after such hard and sore labor, he was offered the bishopric of Rochester, a post he refused. Difficult times ensued, but he courageously bared his breast to the battle. He was censured and shot at through a window, and he suffered as he strove to make the government of Scotland a theocracy during the reign of Mary. We have touched upon his exile in Geneva, where he was greatly influenced by John Calvin, the Genevan Reformer. While there, he published his works against Mary and the tyranny of her court. He returned to Scotland for a while but found it difficult to accomplish much. Receiving a call to a Genevan church, he accepted and, going back, spent the happiest three years of his life there. He, his wife, and their family were greatly honored and loved by all.

Hearing that the fires of Reformation were beginning to burn fiercely in Scotland, and being urged to return, he came back to the Scotland he loved so dearly in 1559, at the age of fifty-four, and gave the remaining thirteen years of his life to the battle of securing her religious liberty. A great and effective door was opened to Knox—and with it many adversaries.

A MAN OF COMBAT

Like the apostle Paul, with whose teachings Knox was saturated, he determined to fight a good fight. Queen Mary, his avowed antagonist, sought to make Scotland entirely Roman Catholic, but the converted priest would have none of it, and he thundered out against idolatry. He broke images, denounced the Mass and false gods, and fought sternly against all Catholic practices.

He Testified Against a Prostituted Royalty

Mary, the young Queen of Scots, was both clever and beautiful. She so fascinated the nobles of her court that they were ready to do anything she willed. She was cruel and devilish, had had several husbands, and was called "Bloody Mary" because of her dark and treacherous deeds against the people. John Knox stood his ground against her and rebuked her sternly. "Who are you," she once said to him, "that presume to school the nobles and sovereign of this realm?" Knox's reply was, "Madam, a subject born within same." In bold terms, he denounced the queen in regard to her marriage to young Darnley, and he was commanded to appear before her at Holyrood Palace to answer for his conduct.

The queen desired that in the future, Knox should tell her privately of anything that he saw to be wrong. When he refused, finding him indifferent to her threats, she tried to conciliate him. Knox was brought to trial for treason but was acquitted. He was, however, forbidden to preach because of the offense given by his sermon on the queen's marriage. This prohibition lasted until the queen's fall in 1567 and the accession of King James.

When Lord Darnley stretched a point, Catholic though he was, and went to hear Knox preach before his trial, the preacher took as his text "Other lords than thou have had dominion over us." He discoursed on God's way of sometimes permitting such lords to be "boys and women" and dwelt on the weakness of Ahab in not controlling his strong-minded queen, Jezebel. The service lasted an hour longer than Darnley had expected, and he flung himself out of the church. Queen Mary and her mother, Mary of Lorraine, feared no other person in all the land as they feared John Knox. "Yon man," the fair Mary cried, after one interview with him, "gart me greet, but grat never tear himself." *Greet* is Scotch for "weep," and what she meant was, "He makes me weep but never weeps himself."

He Testified Against Papal Religion

Having been reared in Roman Catholicism and ordained as a priest, Knox knew all about its inner workings and practices. But, once his eyes were opened and he came, like Martin Luther, to experience justification by faith, he set about purging the land of a debased priesthood—and he lived to see victory. Through his steadfast spirit, Protestantism was confirmed by an act of parliament for Scotland in 1567; the country has remained a stronghold of Presbyterianism ever since. Throughout Christendom, John Knox still lives wherever a Protestant church stands. In fact, an untold number of them bear the honored name of Knox.

A MAN OF COURAGE

Seneca, the ancient Roman philosopher, wrote,

He is a king who fears nothing;
He is a king who will desire nothing.

Knox was a true king in that he feared no one but God and desired nothing save for His glory. Familiar as he was with Scripture, it may be that the Reformer was inspired by the command to the prophet Jeremiah: *"Be not afraid of their faces: for I am with thee to deliver thee, saith the LORD"* (Jeremiah 1:8). Knox neither flattered nor feared anyone. At his burial, Earl Morton, present at the graveside, said of him after the coffin had been lowered, "He lies there who never feared the face of man." The fear of man was a snare Knox avoided. In his darkest hours as a galley slave, he would cheer his fellow prisoners by saying, "Be of good courage. The cause we have is a true one and must and will prosper."

Courageous in life, he was the same in death. After the accession of King James, he spent three years in fruitful service and lived to see better times and to thank God that "the gospel of Jesus Christ is truly and simply preached throughout Scotland." It would seem as if his own preaching became stronger and more tender in his final years. Toward the end, he was so weak that he had to be lifted into the pulpit, "where," says the chronicler, "he had to lean at his first entry; but before he had done with his sermon he was so active and vigorous that he was like to ding the pulpit in blads and fly out of it." The reporter went on to say, "When he entered into the application of his text, he made me so to thrill and tremble that I could not hold a pen to write."

In 1570, Knox was seized with a fit of apoplexy, and although he recovered sufficiently to preach occasionally, he gradually deteriorated. On November 24, 1572, his task was finished. In his last hours, his mind wandered, and he was heard to say that he wanted to go to church and preach on the resurrection of Christ. In one of his conscious moments, he was asked, "Have you hope?" No longer able to speak, he lifted a finger upward and so died. Among his final words was a request to his wife: "Go read where I first cast my anchor," and she read John 17. Before speech finally left him, he softly said, "I praise God for that heavenly sound," and then, with a sigh of relief, he added under his breath, "Now it is come." Thus the stalwart Reformer who never feared an earthly sovereign went home to the ivory palace to see the King he had honored in all His beauty. He was buried on November 26 in the churchyard of Saint Giles, now the courtyard of Parliament House, and only two initials—J. K.—mark the grave of the man who gave Scotland her religious liberty.

The question remains: Are we continuing to reap the fruit of Knox's wonderful labors? Are we standing fast in the religious freedom he gallantly fought for and secured? One wonders what his attitude would be if he could come back to earth and witness the efforts of men to unite into one universal church all denominations and religions, whether Christian or non-Christian. With his uncompromising exposure of the practices of Roman Catholicism, we cannot imagine him having any sympathy with the plans to unify religious bodies accepting the fundamental truths of the gospel with those who reject them, or the merging of the so-called Protestant Church with the Roman Church. We desperately need a man of the caliber of John Knox to foster a spiritual Reformation.

Again, as he died, he asked for the portion of the Word to be read to him in which he had first cast his anchor. Today, the church is drifting. She has failed to cast her anchor in the infallible, unbreakable Word of God, in His infinite love and mercy, in the redeeming grace of Christ, in the everlasting gospel. If only all the energy spent on ecumenicism could be directed into a robust evangelicalism—what a mighty force the church would be in a world of sin and sorrow! After all, the supreme task of Christ's church is soulwinning, for He conceived and commissioned her to go into all the world making disciples, and such an anchor always holds.

CHAPTER 4

ROBERT MURRAY MCCHEYNE: THE YOUNG MINISTER WHO BURNED OUT FOR GOD

In the economy of God, it would seem as if He has honored certain places above others, causing them, because of events and experiences within them, to be sanctified. To mention Bethlehem is to remember the miracle of God becoming flesh. To think of Mount Olivet is to visualize Christ's ministry at such a sacred spot—and His future return to it when He comes to reign. To speak of the place called Calvary is to call to mind the perfect salvation secured there for a sinning race. This is also true of cities and towns of later times, as proven by the historic Scottish city of Dundee.

What has made this city, renowned for its jam and jute, so world famous? Certainly not its industries and its position on the silvery River Tee, but its roll of honor of saintly souls who lived and labored in it. As we have already seen, George Wishart preached

Reformation sermons in Dundee and made it the "Scotch Geneva." In this same city, the great revivalist William Burns was mightily used by God before going to China to accomplish great things for Him. Dundee was the home of Robert Annan, a remarkable saint whose life story has been greatly used. It was also in Dundee that Mary Slessor lived and labored in a jute mill, and from which she went to West Africa to become the uncrowned queen of Calabar.

A host of others less conspicuous, whose lives were fragrant and fruitful for the Master, served Him most faithfully in their day and generation. Our present portrait is of one of Dundee's most holy sons, Robert Murray McCheyne, whose appealing story has been told by many biographers, the greatest spiritual classic being *Memoirs of Robert Murray McCheyne* by Andrew Sonar, his dear friend. From various sources, then, let us try to picture him.

FROM HIS YOUTH UP

Godly influences at home—a most valuable asset—helped to shape his life during his early years. In one sense, he was never much more than a youth, for he died at an early age. The youngest of five, McCheyne was born on May 21, 1813, at 14 Dublin Street in Edinburgh. His father was Adam McCheyne, a man of considerable means and good position. He was also known for his excellent Christian character. As a father, he was firm yet approachable. Robert's mother was Lockhart Murray McCheyne, a very sweet and charming lady who sought to make her home Christ-centered and controlled. After Robert's death, his father, who greatly loved his son and kept all his letters, wrote to a friend, "Robert was from infancy blessed with a sweet, docile, and affectionate temper—a mother's legacy to her child."

It is said that Robert's consuming passion and earnestness when he became a minister influenced his parents to leave their church, where modernism prevailed, and join a more evangelistic one. From infancy, McCheyne was wonderfully endowed both temperamentally and mentally.

His Natural Endowments

As a lad, he was good-looking, attractive, and winsome; very quick in mind and quiet in manner; and the possessor of a fine melodious voice. The description given of David, son of Jesse, can be applied to Robert M. McCheyne: *"He was ruddy and withal of a beautiful countenance and goodly to look to"* (1 Samuel 16:12). There came the day when the latter part of the verse was also applicable to this wonderful youth from a godly home: *"The* Lord *said, Arise and anoint him: for this is he"* (verse 12).

His Scholastic Attainments

McCheyne had a thirst and capacity for knowledge. This can be gleaned from the fact that when he was recovering from the measles, his father taught him the letters of the Greek alphabet. At five, he went to a private school and made great progress, possessing a quick ear and an ability to recite. His instructor said of him, "The child's voice was like a sound from a better life and a better land, so simple and pure." He was so successful that after only a few sessions at his first school, he carried off the second prize.

In October 1821, at the age of eight, he enrolled in the high school in Edinburgh and continued his literary studies there for six years, distinguishing himself in geography and recitation. This gifted scholar was loved by all his companions. One of them gave this tribute: "My recollections are of a tall, slender lad with a sweet, pleasant face, bright yet grave, fond to play, and of a blameless life."

Andrew Bonar says of McCheyne during this period of his life:

> His mind at that time had no relish for any higher joy than
> the refined gaieties of society, and for such pleasures as the

song and the dance could yield. He himself regarded these as days of ungodliness, days wherein he cherished a pure morality, but lived in heart a Pharisee.

Reaching fourteen years of age, he entered Edinburgh University and for almost six years gave himself assiduously to his studies. Although not overly brilliant, he studied languages and gained a few academic honors. He always enjoyed the holidays, which he spent amid natural scenery. Being good with a pencil, he would make sketches of what he saw. He was also an accomplished musician, had considerable knowledge of music, and could sing beautifully. He became a hymnist of no mean order. A few of his hymns were written while he was in Palestine. His best-known hymn is "I Once Was a Stranger to Grace and to God." Others in his collection are "When This Passing World Is Done," "Beneath Moriah's Rocky Side," "When I Stand Before the Throne," "Chosen Not for Good in Me," and "Oft I Walk Beneath the Cloud."

One who often observed young McCheyne said of him as a seventeen-year-old, "A handsome and elegant lad and everything he did seemed to bear the stamp of early culture and native refinement." At twenty, he entered Divinity Hall, Edinburgh, during the winter of 1831. He had experienced no spiritual awakening as yet. While at the university, he had had occasional religious impressions, but none of great depth. During his theological studies, desiring to be useful, he visited the poorer districts of the city on mission work and unconsciously laid the foundation for the great task he was to accomplish in the densely populated parts of Dundee.

His Spiritual Preparation

In spite of his natural qualities and acquired secular and theological knowledge, something deeper was necessary to fashion McCheyne into the saint he would become. The first prompting Godward came when he was eighteen. His brother David, the eldest son of the family, died suddenly at the age of twenty-six after contracting a severe chill. Like his father, Adam, he was a W. S. (Writer of Signet, or lawyer). Before young David died, he had a great spiritual struggle, but peace came at the end. God used this break in the family to bring Robert to his need of Christ, as can be seen in a letter to a friend on July 8, 1842: "This day eleven years ago I lost my loved and loving brother, and began to seek a Brother who cannot die." And, seeking, he soon found Him.

Spiritual progress was slow. Light dawned gradually. Occasionally, Robert would plunge into the gaiety of the world. His conversion was not an instantaneous one, such as Saul of Tarsus experienced. McCheyne himself wrote, "I was led to Christ through deep and ever-abiding, but not awful or distracting, conviction." The book *The Sum of Saving Knowledge* brought him to a clear understanding and acceptance of the way of salvation. Thus, in his diary, March 11, 1834, he wrote, "Read in *The Sum of Saving Knowledge*, the work which I think first of all wrought a change in me. How gladly would I renew the reading of it, if that change might be carried to perfection."

At last he set himself the task of preparing his life's work as "a messenger of grace to guilty men." He started to keep his priceless *Memoirs* and began registering his studies and incidents of his life and work. For instance, we read,

> Sept. 2 – Sabbath Evening. Reading. Too much engrossed, and too little devotional. Preparation for a fall. Warning— we may be too engrossed with the shell even of heavenly things.

> March 12 – Oh, for activity, activity, activity!

> Oct. 17 – Private meditation exchanged for conversation. Here is the root of the evil—forsake God and He forsakes us.

These *Memoirs*, edited by Dr. Andrew Bonar, are incomparable among devotional reading for the heart and should be in every Christian's library.

A GOOD MINISTER OF JESUS CHRIST

Paul's wish and prayer for young Timothy, his son in the faith, can certainly be ascribed to Robert Murray McCheyne, who set out to equip himself in every way for the work of the ministry. After finishing his theological studies, he was licensed on July 1, 1835, to preach. He went to Annan, where his relatives were known, and preached before the Presbytery there. He so became, as he himself expressed it, "A preacher of the gospel, an honor to which I cannot name an equal." He had a most solemn sense of his calling, evident from his statement that "the pulpit is a wonderful place....God comes nigh you there when you cast yourself upon Him and His help." Is this not the secret of spiritual power in preaching the Word? McCheyne scorned any ambition to star as a popular pulpiteer. His burning passion was to be a pastor according to God's heart, feeding the saints with knowledge and understanding. (See Jeremiah 3:15.)

At Duniface

McCheyne's first charge was in the village of Duniface, about three miles from Larbet. He went to assist the Rev. John Bonar, minister of the Parish of Larbert and brother of the renowned Andrew Bonar. Here the young preacher remained for almost a year. As his duties were light, he gave himself to much prayer and to the study of the Bible in its original languages, as well as to the reading of the works of Jonathan Edwards, Samuel Rutherford, and other saintly men. His preaching at this time was of an experimental nature, dealing with the inner life of the believer. There also came a passion to convert sinners. "Enlarge my heart and I shall preach," he prayed, and God enlarged his heart. He grasped every opportunity to spread the glorious evangel. He once passed a band of gypsies sitting around a campfire, and he sat down with them and spoke to them on the parable of the lost sheep. Recording this incident in his diary, he said, "The children were attentive and the old people touched a little."

Much time was also consumed visiting the sinful and the sick. When weary and disappointed, he would plead with God for "gales of spiritual life," and when refreshed, he would continue to perform his manifold labors. His short ministry came to a close in August 1836, and he left many behind in Duniface who blessed God for the influence of his life and labors.

At Dundee

McCheyne's second and last charge was in this important Scottish city. A new church, Saint Peter's, was seeking a minister. McCheyne was asked to preach as a candidate, and on August 14, 1836, he preached three times. In the morning, his message was on "The Sower." In the afternoon, he preached on "The Voice of the Beloved." In the evening, he spoke on "Ruth the Moabitess."

Borne along by the Spirit, the young minister preached with all his heart, and souls were blessed that day through his witness. By a large majority he was called, and on November 24, 1836, he was ordained as minister of the new church. His first sermon was on the words of Isaiah, *The Spirit of the Lord God is upon me; because the Lord hath anointed me to preach good tidings*" (Isaiah 61:1). Said the preacher, "May this be prophetic of the object of my coming here," and it was, for he never failed to function as God's messenger in God's message.

His first description of Dundee was somewhat severe: "A city given to idolatry and hardness of heart. I fear there is much of what Isaiah speaks of: 'The prophets prophesy lies, and the people love to have it so.'" Interceding for the city, he prayed that "this city of chimney pots might be changed into the garden of the Lord."

The first months at this new charge were arduous and trying. The membership numbered eleven hundred, a task by no means easy, as our glimpse of his six-year ministry there will prove. A fatal attack of influenza struck the city, and McCheyne found it hard to cope with the visitation of the sick and dying.

A PREACHER

McCheyne loved to preach—and he could preach! From the outset, the church was full at all services; people were attracted from the city and countryside to hear his heart-searching messages. Well over a thousand regularly attended, crowding the aisles and pulpit stairs. Because of his growing fame, calls to larger and wealthier charges reached him, but, believing that Dundee was the will of God for him, he remained there. He wrote to his beloved mother, "Dear Mamma, You must just make up your mind to let me be murdered among the lanes of Dundee, instead of seeing me fattening on the green glebe of Skirling"—one of the places that desired him. His preaching was never commonplace. He studied earnestly and refused to be interrupted when preparing his sermons. Often he would ride out "to the ruined church of Invergowrie to enjoy an hour's perfect solitude." There were two conspicuous aspects of his powerful and fruitful preaching:

His Preaching Was Analytical

His messages were simple and lucid, clear and plain. Prominent as a textual preacher, as his printed sermons show, he kept close to Scripture. He was once asked if he had any fear that he would run dry. His reply was, "When the Bible runs dry, then I shall."

His Preaching Was Passionate

McCheyne not only knew all about the *art* of preaching; he felt the *heart* of it, as well: "He was often in an agony till he should see Christ formed in the hearts of his people," and this gave his pulpit discourses a love and compassion that compelled results. He spent much time pleading with God for men before he went forth to plead with men for God. One who knew him well wrote,

> He was one of the most complete ministers I ever met. He was a great preacher, an excellent visitor, a full-orbed saint. He visited the dying on Saturdays that his heart might be thrilled by what he saw, and that he might be put into an arrested and serious frame for Sabbath work.

AN EVANGELIST

Ever faithful to his own church, he became, in practice, the evangelist of Forfarshire. He found it hard to refuse an invitation to preach. He believed in scattering the light while the candle of his life burned on. At one time, he embarked on an evangelistic tour of the north of Scotland and preached incessantly for three weeks. Some came to stone him—and ended up entreating him to stay. One who had cast mud at him wept later on when hearing of his death. McCheyne's passionate preaching made sinners afraid. He often preached in Ireland, and during the last months of his life, he was often away spreading the flame. Once, he preached in Ruthwell to a vast crowd in the marketplace on the topic "The Great White Throne." He closed his message saying that they would never meet again on earth—and they never did.

A MISSIONARY

Like the Master he dearly loved and so faithfully served, McCheyne believed that there were "other sheep" that must be brought into the fold; his was a missionary heart. From the time his soul was awakened, he was eager to visit the regions beyond. He had a great love for the Jews. In 1838, when his medical friends advised a change when he was suffering from ill health, he went to Palestine to undertake as a mission of inquiry among the Jews both in Palestine and on the Continent. To a Christ-loving soul like his, the Holy Land was full of the sweetest, most tender interest. His poetic descriptions of this sacred spot are without parallel. Wherever he met Jews, he would repeat texts in Hebrew and pray for their salvation. His report on what he saw greatly increased general interest in the work among God's ancient people.

While he was absent, William Burns substituted for him, and under his preaching at Saint Peter's, a remarkable revival broke out. When McCheyne returned, he was overwhelmed with joy and entered into the stirring work, which continued until the close of his life.

A REVIVALIST

Throughout his ministry in Dundee, McCheyne was one of the chief instruments in Scotland in promoting evangelical revival. He strongly felt that modernism, worldliness, and carnal policy in the church were foes of the gospel. While he was in Hamburg, he heard of the revival under Burns, and he could not return to his church quickly enough, for this was what his heart hungered for. Doubtless this divine visitation was the fruit of his perpetual intercession and ceaseless toil. He found his church "a Bochim, a place of tears" (see Judges 2:1, 5), for whole families were affected, with people falling to the ground groaning and crying for mercy. The Word of God grew and multiplied, and the fire that was kindled in Dundee spread throughout Scotland. Both Burns and McCheyne went here and there as two flaming revivalists. "The battle is beginning," they said. "The enemy will not give way without a struggle." McCheyne's *Diary* is full of what God wrought during this time. Here is one item:

> April 5. Sabbath. Spoke to 24 young persons, one by one; almost all affected about their souls. Alas! spiritual dearth prevails today, and our churches need another Holy Ghost revival such as swept Scotland over 130 years ago.

A SAINT

Writing to a young student, McCheyne gave him this counsel: "Above all, keep much in the presence of God. Never see the face of man till you have seen His face who is our life and all." And he practiced what he preached, for he desired above all things a holy walk and manner, and always cultivated his own spiritual life. He longed for "a deeper peace and holier walk." His prime concern was the nurture of his own soul, and so he wrote, "I ought to pray before seeing anyone....I feel it is better to rise early and begin with God...to see His face first, to get my soul near Him before it is near another." McCheyne learned the secret of perfecting holiness in the Lord. Is it any wonder, then, that he left such an impact on the lives of multitudes? The most effective instrument in the hand of God is a holy life, as the record of this famous Presbyterian minister proves.

FINISHING THE RACE

The later years of McCheyne's life were marked by growth in holiness and likeness to the Lord. As he neared heaven, he became more heavenly in spirit and demeanor. His health had always been delicate and fragile, for he had contracted tuberculosis. Yet, in spite of his fragility, he labored on, never acknowledging defeat. One day, he wrote to his mother, "My cough is turned into a loose kind of grumble, like the falling down of a shower of stones in a quarry." He never married. During his swift and strenuous days in Dundee, he was lovingly cared for by his sister Eliza, whom he addressed thusly: "How art thou thyself, my own Deaconness and Helpmeet of thy poor brother?"

Even though the valiant warrior felt his lamp was burning low and the end of the battle was near, he did not relax. On October 5, a Sabbath, he preached three times. The following Sabbath, he spoke to his own people morning and afternoon, and then, at night, he preached in nearby Broughty Ferry on "Arise, shine, for thy light is come!" (See Isaiah 60:1.) How prophetic this was to be for him. Although typhus fever was prevalent in the district, this tireless evangelist did not screen himself but visited the afflicted. Because of his poor physical condition and lack of resistance, he caught the infection and succumbed. On Wednesday, October 22, his parents and Andrew Bonar were sent for. A friend who visited him lamented that he was not in the pulpit, and McCheyne answered, "I am preaching the sermon God would have me do." This was his last conscious message. His sister quoted Cowper's hymn, saying, "Sometimes the light surprises the Christian as he sings."

In his delirium, at times he prayed, "This parish, Lord, this people, this whole place." Then he would break out in pleas with sinners to repent. This delirious condition continued until Saturday morning, March 25, 1843, when he lifted up his hands in a benediction and, without a sigh or pang, went home to the bosom of God. He was under thirty years of age when he finished his race, and people spoke of his premature end. Yet, in the will of God, his death was not untimely. God never makes a mistake when a young saint is removed.

> Oh sir! the good die first,
> And they whose hearts are dry as summer's dust
> Burn to the socket.[3]

McCheyne had finished his course, even although a short one, and so God took him. The following Lord's Day was a dark one at St. Peter's. Throngs of congregants mourned the passing of their beloved pastor. Says the historian, "All Dundee was moved, and the day of his funeral was one of the greatest and most subduing in the annals of the city." Robert's father yielded to the request that his son's body should rest alongside the church in which he had been so signally used of God and so dearly loved.

---

3. William Wordsworth, *Excursion* (book 1), 1814.

Even though dead, Robert Murray McCheyne still speaks. Although he was in the ministry for only some six years and died at twenty-nine, his is an abiding influence. We are apt to forget that it is not the *length* of life that counts but the *quality* of it.

> We live in deeds, not years; in thoughts, not breaths;
>> In feelings, not in figures on a dial.
> We should count time by heart-throbs.
>> He most lives
> Who thinks most—feels the noblest—acts the best.[4]

While some of his sermons and poems are in print, he published no books and took little part in public movements. He died young, yet his story has traveled the world over. One item in his precious diary reads, "O God for grace to live that when dead, I shall be missed!" How deeply he was missed! Age after age has risen to call him blessed. Dr. Bonar's *Memoirs and Diary of Robert Murray McCheyne* has been used for the conversion of many. Although he has been in the ivory palaces now for some 130 years, his garments still have the fragrance of myrrh, cassia, and aloes. As one writer has expressed it, "McCheyne's beautiful Christian life is an example to aspiring believers and a rebuke to desponding sluggards."

Jesus said to His disciples, *"Learn of me"* (Matthew 11:29). What are some of the outstanding traits of McCheyne's life from which we can learn much? In what ways has he left an example to follow?

His Sense of Sin

In his most moving hymn, H. Twells bids us remember that

> None, O Lord, have perfect rest,
> For none are wholly free from sin;

---

4. Philip James Bailey, "We Live in Deeds, Not Years."

> And they who fain would serve Thee best
> Are conscious most of wrong within.[5]

The many entries in McCheyne's diary prove this was true of him. One day he wrote, "The lust of praise has ever been my besetting sin." He was vastly popular, with a physical beauty that satisfied the eye and a personality that commanded attention, and it must have been hard for him to resist admiration. After his death, his father said that he could understand why his son's life had been cut short. It was to prevent the townsfolk making an idol of him. A tenth part of the popularity accorded McCheyne has puffed up and ruined many a minister. But, conscious of his failing, young Robert tried to mortify self and lay in dust life's glory, dead. Under the date July 7, Sabbath, we read in his diary:

> Two things that defile this day in looking back are love of praise running through all, and consenting to listen to worldly talk at all.

On another day we find an entry revealing his deep sense of sin:

> None but God knows what an abyss of corruption is in my heart.

Would that we could always be aware that in us, apart from grace, there dwelleth no good thing!

His Walk with God

In spite of his constant care of over a thousand members, he made time to feed his inner fires. His diary abounds with references to the hours he spent in secret prayer. A friend of McCheyne's wrote, "During the last years of his short life he walked calmly in almost unbroken fellowship with the Father and the Son." His constant incentive to a holy walk was the truth of the return of Christ. How he loved the thought of His appearing! Scotland

---

5. Henry Twells, "At Even, When the Sun Was Set," 1868.

never had a saintlier man than Robert Murray McCheyne. He lived a God-centered life. He had no other interest in life except the glory of God. To his soul, God was the center and circumference of all things.

His Passion for Souls

Living so near the Savior, McCheyne caught something of His passion and compassion for the lost; therefore, he was extremely active in plucking brands from the burning. One day, while standing by a fireman fighting the flames, he said to the man, "Does that fire remind you of anything?" Like Livingstone of Shotts, he often preached "as out of the very heart of the Weeper of Olivet." Another diary entry reads, "O, when will I plead with my tears and inward yearnings over sinners?" The church's tragedy today is her possession of far too many passionless pastors whose eyes never run down with rivers of water for the destruction of God's people. (See Lamentations 3:48–49.) They know so little of what it is "to weep o'er the erring one, and lift up the fallen." One Monday, McCheyne met his dear friend Andrew Bonar and said to him, "What did you preach on yesterday?" Bonar replied in all solemnity, "Hell!" McCheyne replied, "Were you able to preach it with tears?"

His Loyalty to Scripture

While the modernistic approach to the Bible was not as prominent in McCheyne's day as it is today, yet there was a movement in the direction of doubt as to its divine inspiration and veracity. Because of his reverence for the Word as a divine revelation, he was mightily used of God. How can a preacher achieve victories with a blunt sword? Dundee's renowned saint always read Scripture, first of all for his own edification, and then for the spiritual benefit of others. He took his stand upon Scripture—authoritative, all through—and found any part of it he preached on as being "*quick, powerful, and sharper than any two edged sword"* (Hebrews 4:12). As a result, his church was crowded with eager listeners, and it continued to be that way.

Such, then, is the portrait of the short life of one who burned out serving the Lord whom he loved with an intense passion. He lived and labored so as to be missed when his eyelids closed in death. We read of Jehoram, who departed this life *"without being desired"* (2 Chronicles 21:20). Because of the pernicious influence of his character, it was better for his contemporaries that he was dead. How different it was with McCheyne, and with all who serve the Lord as faithfully as he did!

> I would be missed when gone
> I would not—my life done
> Have no eyes wet for me,
> No hearts touch'd tenderly,
> No good of me confessed;
> Dead—and yet not missed.

CHAPTER 5

DAVID LIVINGSTONE: THE SCOT WHO LIGHTED A DARK CONTINENT

It is debatable whether any nationality has contributed more outstanding missionaries, theologians, preachers, and writers to the cause of Christ than the Scottish. As the result of the Reformation under John Knox, there emerged a host of men of culture and sturdy caliber, each of whom left footprints behind them on the sands of time. The picture gallery of Scottish church history is crowded with magnificent portraits. For instance, when we read *Bible Characters*, we think of Alexander Whyte; and when we sing "O Love That Wilt Not Let Me Go," the image of the famous blind preacher George Matheson comes before us.

In the missionary room of the Scottish picture gallery, no portrait is as prominent as that of David Livingstone, who carried the light of Christian civilization to the world's most backward area, and who remains one of the world's most intrepid missionaries. He joined Barnabas and Paul in hazarding his life for the name of the Lord Jesus Christ. Youth of today should be persuaded to read the record of Scotland's noble son. His life and labors reveal what God is able to accomplish through one wholly committed to Him. Livingstone certainly knew what it was to climb the steep ascent to heaven through peril, toil, and pain.

THE BLANTYRE YOUTH

The early years of Livingstone have never ceased to fascinate the hearts and grip the attention of the young with a desire to serve the Lord. His thrilling story inspired the factory girl Mary Slessor and helped to stir within her a longing to work in heathen lands. The facts of his young days have been told a thousand times or more. This Clydesdale lad was brought up in a tenement house in Blantyre. The home was a Bible-loving one, a factor that wielded a formative influence over his life and laid the foundation of his monumental work.

His father was Neil Livingstone, whom a friend described as "a man of great spiritual earnestness and his whole life was consecrated to duty and the fear of God." Would that the world had more fathers with the same reputation! He was a deacon in the Independent Church in Hamilton, a member of the local missionary society, and an earnest Temperance worker. He was also a great reader and acted as an unpaid colporteur. For a living, he traveled the countryside selling tea. His income was meager, and the family had to live sparingly.

David's mother, Agnes Hunter Livingstone, was remembered as being "active, orderly, and of thorough cleanliness." She trained her family in the same virtues. She was a delicate little woman with a wonderful flow of good spirits. She was remarkable for the beauty of the eyes, and her son David's bore a strong resemblance. Neil and Agnes were married in 1810 and resided first in Glasgow, removing later to Blantyre. Five sons, two of whom died in infancy, and two daughters were born to this commendable pair. David often recalled his mother's love, care, and thrift. She died June 18, 1865, but lived long enough to share the triumphs of her illustrious, much-loved son. In his *Journal*, Monday, June 19, Livingstone wrote,

> When going away in 1858, she said to me that she would have liked one of her laddies to lay her head in the grave. It so happened that I was there to pay the last tribute to a dear good mother.

What a tremendous asset a godly home is! If, in the goodness of God you have one, be sure to respect and value it.

On March 19, 1813, David was born in that poor, humble, yet lovely home in Blantyre, Lanarkshire, Scotland. As a young man, I served as an evangelist with the Lanarkshire Christian Union and often preached in Blantyre. Whenever I was there, I would visit the old Livingstone home, which has been preserved as a memorial. The tenement buildings, so familiar in those days, and existing to this day in slum areas, were made of two-roomed flats. They were called "But 'n a' Ben." *But* is the Scotch for "kitchen," while *ben* means "within" or "inner" and was used to designate a kind of parlor off the kitchen. In the *but*, or kitchen, there were usually two recesses built out from the wall that served as beds. These recesses were sometimes called "a hole in the wall," for that is what they looked like. In one of the *buts*, Livingstone first saw the light of day. When my wife and I were married, in Motherwell, near Blantyre, we set up house in a "But 'n a' Ben," and our son was born in one of these kitchen *buts*.

Livingstone was named David after David Hunter, his mother's father. The compelling name Livingstone has suggested several things to those who loved the missionary. Professor George Wilson, acknowledging a book David Livingstone had sent him in 1857, wrote expressively, "May your name be propitious: in all your long and weary journeys may the *Living* half of your name outweight the other: till after long and blessed labors the white *Stone* is given you in the happy land." After his death, a very sweet eulogy appeared, of all places, in *Punch*, the last verse of which ran:

> He needs no epitaph to guard a name
> Which men shall prize while worthy work is known.
> He lived and died for good—be that his fame:
> Let marble crumble: this is LIVING – STONE.

There is little to say about his earliest days. He helped his mother with household chores. He always insisted that his mother would lock the door so that no school chums could come in and make fun of him. As a child, he was calm and self-reliant. At the age of nine, he received a present of a New Testament from his Sunday school teacher for repeating Psalm 119, with its 176 verses, on two successive evenings with only five errors—proof that perseverance was bred in his bones. He was very fond of reading travel books and would always go with his father to missionary meetings to hear missionaries relate their adventures.

Factory Life

Because Livingstone's parents were poor, he began to work in a neighboring factory to help out with the home finances. All the children had to work, for the mother was not able to feed and clothe them all on her husband's meager earnings. At ten years of age, David entered the Blantyre Mill and began as a "piecer," and at the age of nineteen, he became a "spinner." He had to work fourteen hours a day, from six in the morning till eight at night. To his mother's delight, he put the first two shillings he earned—six pence—in her lap. She gave him back a little of it, and he used the amount to purchase a secondhand Latin grammar. From an early age, he evinced a thirst for knowledge. Later on in his life, he was to write of those hard days,

> The dictionary part of my labors was followed up till midnight or later, if my mother did not interfere by jumping up and snatching the books out of my hand. I had to be back to the factory by six in the morning and continue my work with intervals for breakfast and dinner till eight at night. I read in this way classical works, and knew Virgil and Horace better at sixteen than I do now.

His method was to place a book on his machine and read in his spare moments. Livingstone never hid the fact of his hard, poor life. Years later, when the highest in the land showered compliments upon him, he wrote to a friend about "my own order, the honest poor." On the gravestone of his parents were their names and the names of their children who had died, along with the phrase "Children of Poor and Pious Parents." What a rebuke the perseverance of those factory days is to much of the indolent youth today! The prevailing spirit seems to say, "Work as little as you can for as much as you can get."

University Life

During the winter of 1836–1837, David Livingstone entered Glasgow University. In the summer months, he worked in the mill, and the wages he earned supported him during the winter months at the university. He lived sparingly and cut down his spending to the lowest. Glasgow is some fifteen miles from Blantyre, and he would walk there and back. He received his degree in medicine in 1840 and then undertook theological studies at Edinburgh University. Speaking at the centenary of Livingstone, Dr. John Clifford said of him, "He had many teachers, and we remember how the teaching of his parents helped in molding him for after years. His home was poor, but it was the household of saints.

Luxury was not there, but the Word of God was there. His toil was bitter, but no bitter word escaped his lips because his parents had sent him to these early labors."

Christian Life

Livingstone had a consuming desire to be a medical missionary, hence his university studies, but he was not able to trace any exact spiritual crisis whereby he became the Lord's. Reared in a godly home, he had a Christian consciousness from earliest childhood and knew that he was the Lord's. It would seem as if he owed his spiritual impetus to Dr. Thomas Dick, of Broughty Ferry, whose book on *The Philosophy of a Future State* pointed out some of his errors and showed him the way of salvation. When he was about twenty years old, he passed through a deep experience, of which he wrote years later:

> I saw the duty and inestimable privilege immediately to accept salvation by Christ. Humbly believing that through sovereign grace and mercy I have been enabled to do so, and having felt in some measure its effects on my still depraved and deceitful heart, it is my desire to show my attachment to the cause of Him who died for me by devoting my life to His service.

Without such a solid spiritual foundation, Livingstone would never have become the renowned missionary-explorer God made him. He believed he had been saved to serve. Far too many who are not saved seek to serve.

THE AFRICAN MISSIONARY

When the young medical-missionary set out for darkest Africa, he had no idea of the trials and triumphs that would be his before he died on his knees in a lonely hut. Little did this handsome, well-built youth, shy and ill-at-ease in public, realize what fame would be his.

His First Missionary Impulse

At first, Livingstone had no direct thought of being a missionary, although he felt his responsibility in this direction. "Feeling that the salvation of men ought to be the chief desire and aim of every Christian," he made this resolution: "That he would give to the cause of missions all that he might earn beyond what was required for his subsistence." Having such a missionary enthusiast as a father must have influenced young David in the direction of the regions beyond. It would seem, however, that his first definite decision to be a missionary came through Dr. Karl Gatzlaff, the German Apostle to China, of whose work Livingstone had read and heard so much. He decided to offer himself for work in China when he was only twenty-one. "The claims of so many millions of his fellow-creatures, and the complaints of the scarcity of qualified missionaries," made China his first love, and "his efforts were constantly directed toward that object without any fluctuation." But, owing to the Opium War raging at that time, the door into China was closed.

His Definite Call to Africa

While engaged in his theological studies at Edinburgh, David went out on his first preaching engagement. But when he rose to speak, words failed him. "Friends, I have forgotten all I had to say," he gasped, and then in shame he came down from the pulpit. Dr. Robert Moffat was in the city at the time, after having established a mission in Kuraman, South Africa. Meeting David in the moment of his discouragement, he advised him not to give up, telling him that perhaps God wanted him to be a doctor instead of a preacher. But the young student was determined to be both, and a missionary besides. There is no doubt that Livingstone owed his entrance into Africa to Robert Moffat, who was to become his father-in-law. Moffat himself described the interview with the young man so desirous of serving the Lord abroad:

By and by he asked me whether I thought he would do for Africa. I said I believed he would, if he would go not to an old station, but advance to unoccupied ground, specifying the vast plain to the north, where I had sometimes seen, in the morning sun, the smoke of a 1,000 villages, where no missionary had ever been. At last Livingstone said, "What is the use of my waiting for the end of this abominable opium war. I will go at once to Africa!" The Directors concurred, and Africa became his sphere.

Thus, in 1838, the London Missionary Society accepted his application. He had fully counted the cost of his decision to go to Africa, evident from his own statement: "The hardships and dangers of missionary life, so far as I have had the means of ascertaining their nature and extent, have been the subject of serious reflection, and in dependence on the promised assistance of the Holy Spirit, I have no hesitation in saying that I would willingly submit to them, considering my constitution capable of enduring any ordinary share of hardship and fatigue."

His Departure for the Field

The last night in the old Blantyre home that he dearly loved was a sad one. Father and son sat up late discussing missions. The next morning, November 17, 1840, the family rose at five, and his mother prepared breakfast for all, after which David conducted family worship, reading Psalms 121 and 135. He then prayed, commending one and all to God. Sorrowful farewells over, father and son left the humble home and walked the fifteen miles to Glasgow, where David caught the Liverpool steamer at Broomielaw. At the quay, they looked into each other's faces for the last time on earth— for, in the will of God, they never met again. The noble old man walked slowly back to Blantyre with a lonely heart, no doubt, yet praising God for a son he could give to Africa. As for David, his face was now set in earnest toward the Dark Continent, where he was to give his life accomplishing great things for God.

Livingstone was twenty-eight years when he sailed on December 8, 1840, aboard the *George* for distant shores. To an old companion, he wrote, "I want my life to be spent as profitably as a pioneer as in any other way." Livingstone took as his motto, "I am ready to go anywhere, provided it be forward!" And forward he went, into the darkness of the unknown, as a messenger of Him who came to banish darkness in a world of sin.

While he was on his way home for his first furlough, he heard news of his father's death when upon reaching Cairo. He arrived in England on December 9, 1856, and then learned of his father's great desire to see him again. "You wished so much to see David," said his daughter to David's father as his life was ebbing away. "Aye, very much, very much," he replied, "but the will of the Lord be done."

The first thing David did when he reached the home of sorrow was to sit in his father's empty chair. This experience moved him deeply. One of his sisters wrote later to a friend:

> The first evening he asked all about father's illness and death. One of us remarked that he knew he was dying and his spirits seemed to rise. David burst into tears. At family worship that evening he said with deep feeling—"We bless Thee, O Lord, for our parents. We give Thee thanks for the dead who have died in the Lord."

His First Sphere

Livingstone first spent time in the Bechuana Country, Central Africa, where he developed a burning compassion for the native peoples. Entering a tribe, he would make friends with the chieftain, treat the sick, and preach to the natives about a God who became the heavenly Father of all who trusted Him. The traffic in slaves shocked and saddened his heart, and he vowed that he would dedicate his life to stamping out such an evil. Because of the way his healing medicines relieved people, and because he taught about a better way of living, he earned the title "The Good One." One who observed Livingstone in those initial years wrote of him, "His marvelous qualities became manifest even before he had mastered any of the native languages. The chiefs recognized in him a man of noble character, tender sympathy, and infinite helpfulness."

His Marriage

For the first four years of his missionary career, Livingstone was a bachelor, with no thought of marriage, feeling that it was best to be free. Then he came to realize that perhaps marriage would aid him in the tasks ahead. He had contact with the Kuruman Mission, where the Moffats labored, on their return from furlough. He visited their home, and one day beneath the fruit trees, he proposed to Mary, the daughter of Dr. and Mrs. Robert Moffat. Having been born in Africa, Mary was used to the hardships and dangers of the jungle and desert and was a fit companion for the pioneer missionary-doctor. A few months later, they married, and they were very happy, although they often separated because Mary was not strong enough for the hard life of trekking through trackless jungles. In the course of time, there were three little children at her skirts, and she decided to stay at a mission center, care for her bairns, and pray for her husband as he pressed tirelessly on. Both husband and wife were united in putting Christ first. Here is a heart-moving extract from a letter David wrote to Mary:

And now, my dearest, farewell. May God bless you! Let your affections be towards Him much more than towards me: and kept by His mighty power and grace, I hope I shall never give you cause to regret that you have given me a part. Whatever friendship we feel towards each other, let us always look to Jesus as our Common Friend and Guide, and may He shield you with His everlasting arms from all evil.

Both of them returned to England to bring their three children to be educated in the country. After a while, they journeyed back to Africa, very lonely without their children. Little did those young children know they would not see their beloved mother again. On April 21, 1862, Mary became ill, and on Sunday, April 27, the end came. The heart-stricken husband "was sitting by the side of a rude bed formed of boxes; but covered with a soft mattress, on which lay his dying wife," and he held her close as she breathed her last. "The man who had faced so many deaths, and braved so many dangers, was now utterly broken down and weeping like a child" over the passing of his Mary. He buried her beneath a large baobab tree at Shupanga, there to await the resurrection morn.

What a touching scene that must have been, as the bereaved husband found himself alone in vast Africa! Yet "solitude is the mother country of the strong." Livingstone deeply felt the loss of his wife. His *Journal* contains many references to her: "It is the first heavy stroke I have suffered, and quite takes away my strength. I wept over her who well deserved many tears. I loved her when I married her, and the longer I lived with her I loved her the more. God pity the children, who were all tenderly attached to her, and I am left alone in the world by one whom I felt to be part of myself." On May 11, he wrote, "My dear, dear Mary has been this evening a fortnight in heaven—absent from the body, present with the Lord." On May 31, "The loss of my ever dear Mary lies like a heavy weight on my heart." A year later, April 27, 1863, this item appears in his *Journal*: "On this day twelve months ago, my beloved Mary Moffat was removed from me by death."

Familiar as he was with the poets, doubtless the words of Tennyson brought comfort to his empty heart:

If I can, I'll come again, mother,
from out my resting place:
Though you'll not see me, mother,
I shall look upon your face;
Though I cannot speak a word,
I shall hearken what you say,
And be often, often with you when you think
I'm far away.

THE INTREPID EXPLORER

Although Livingstone became world-renowned for his explorations, he retained his missionary zeal. Writing home to his brother Charles, he said, "I am a missionary, heart and soul. God had an only Son, and He became a missionary and a physician. A poor, poor imitation of Him I am, or wish to be. In this service I hope to live, in it I wish to die."

Afterward he severed his connection with the London Missionary Society and spent the last years of his life exploring what were then the unknown parts of the dark continent of Africa. He became, as one put it, "Traveler, geographer, zoologist, astronomer, missionary, physician, and mercantile director; did ever man sustain so many characters at once? Or did ever man perform the duties of each with such painstaking accuracy and so great success?"

In his article on Livingstone in *Reader's Digest*, O. K. Armstrong wrote,

His feats of exploration rank with the greatest. Exploring one-third of a huge Continent—from the Cape almost to the Equator and from the Atlantic to the Indian Ocean— he opened up a vaster unknown area of the earth's surface than any other single man. He charted all the regions he visited and sent precise reports to the Royal Geographical

Society, London. He was the first European to find the
Great Lake Ngami. He came upon some magnificent falls,
more than twice as high as Niagara, and named them
Victoria Falls in honor of his Queen.

He traveled some twenty-nine thousand miles in Africa and
added to the then-known part of the globe about a million square
miles. His friend Maclear, the Astronomer Royal at the Cape, to
whom his observations were regularly forwarded for verification
and correction, said, "Such a man deserves every encouragement
in the power of his country to give. He has done that which few
other travelers in Africa can boast of—he has fixed his geographical points with great accuracy, and yet he is only a poor missionary."

His Sacrificial Labors

What a striking parallel there is between the many sufferings of Livingstone as he pursued his missionary and exploration
activities and the numerous perils of another indomitable pioneer-
missionary—the apostle Paul. The African explorer knew what it
was to be *"in journeyings often,"* and to experience the hardships
of being *"in weariness and painfulness, in watchings often, in hunger
and thirst, in fastings often, in cold and nakedness"* (2 Corinthians
11:26–27). When we compare the "peril, toil, and pain" others
have endured for Christ's sake with our easy life and lack of suffering, we feel somewhat ashamed.

> Must I be carried to the skies
> On flowery beds of ease,
> While others fought to win the prize
> And sailed through bloody seas?[6]

Livingstone was often in peril. The entire world knows about
the thrilling story of his encounter with a lion at Mabotsa. The
animal seized him by the shoulder, tore his flesh, and crushed his

6. Isaac Watts, "Am I a Soldier of the Cross?" 1721.

bone. He would have been killed, had not his life been miraculously saved by a native teacher who was supported by a lady in England for twelve pounds a year. This native was one of his converts, and Livingstone had chosen him as his first native superintendent of schools. He succeeded in drawing the lion away. Never again was the missionary able to lift that arm above his head without pain. Exposed at all times, not only against wild beasts but also savage men, Livingstone had no fear. The hardy preacher's endurance and scorn of danger became legendary.

In his toil and travel, he became subject to fevers and also apprehensive of them, seeing that his beloved Mary had died from a fever. His work as a doctor was vitally important to his preaching. In caring for the bodies of the sick, he was able to reach their hearts for Christ. Daily he demonstrated the use of quinine in treating malaria. For the first five years of his work in Africa, he himself had thirty-one attacks of fever. Without quinine, he would have died. With it, he revived whole families and tribes. Writing to his sister about a new venture he had embarked on, he said,

> Fever may cut us all off. I feel much when I think of the children dying. But who will go if we don't. Not one. I would venture everything for Christ. Pity I have so little to give. But He will accept me for He is a good Master. Never one like Him. He can sympathize. May He forgive, and purify and bless us.

One of the most trying facets of a missionary's life is isolation. Being cut off from home and dear ones and all the comforts and amenities of civilization is not an easy cross to carry. Livingstone had a full share of loneliness, as extracts from his *Journal* prove. Before his wife died, he deeply felt his separation from her and their children. Many of his letters to his much-loved Mary, at whose grave he lingered for several days, are too sacred to spread before the public. But here is a brief paragraph from one of them:

How I miss you now, and the children! My heart yearns
incessantly over you....Take them all around you, and kiss
them for me. Tell them I have left them for the love of
Jesus, and they must love Him too, and avoid sin, for that
displeases Jesus.

While Livingstone's medical knowledge and supplies proved
valuable to him amid his physical sufferings, there were yet times
when pain and sickness were hard to bear. An item in his *Journal*
reads, "Very ill from bleeding from the bowels and purging. Bled
all night. Got up at 1 a.m. to take latitude." Attempting a new
journey with his native helpers, he had to cut the way through
trees and jungle thorns, and he must have presented a pitiable
sight. Writing of this experience in his *Journal*, he said, "With our
hands all raw and bloody, and knees through trousers, we at length
emerged." Livingstone had to tear his handkerchief in two to tie
over his cut knees.

In 1869, he took ill with a severe case of pneumonia. He was
on the memorable expedition to discover the sources of the Nile
so that European trade might come from the north to the interior
of Africa. He was ill much of the time. Unfriendly savages stole
his supplies. Many of his helpers deserted him. Incessant rains
and tsetse flies made travel almost impossible, and he succumbed.
Faithful natives carried him on a rough litter for the two month
trek to Lake Tanganyika for rest and treatment.

His *Journal* from 1867 ends with a statement about the scarcity of food and the physical weakness that ensued. There was
nothing to eat but the coarsest grain of the country. He began his
Journal for 1868 with a prayer that if he should die that year, he
might be prepared for it. Describing his difficulties in a humorous
way in a letter to his daughter, he said, "I broke my teeth tearing
at the maize and other hard food, and they are coming out. One
front tooth is out, and I have such an awful mouth. If you expect a
kiss from me, you may take it through a speaking trumpet."

His Encounter with Stanley

Livingstone spent more than two years recuperating from his emaciated condition at Lake Tanganyika. During this time, nothing was heard of him in Britain, and much concern was felt about his welfare. On every hand, this question was being asked: "Where is Livingstone?" Two relief expeditions were organized and sent out to find him, but both parties had to return because of tropical diseases. Then the enterprising manager of the *New York Herald* sensed the possibility of a great story of this missionary-doctor-explorer *lost* in the heart of Africa. The manager was James Gordon Bennett. He commissioned star reporter Henry Morton Stanley, the twenty-nine-year-old foreign correspondent of the *Herald*, to go to Africa and find Livingstone, no matter how long it took or how much money it cost. Reaching Zanzibar, Stanley assembled a party of almost two hundred carriers to transport the loads of goods and medicines the *Herald* had supplied.

But Stanley was to experience some of the hardship of the man he had set out to seek. There were those who tried to kill him, and malaria and dysentery wore him down. Because of torrential rains, progress was slow. "Yet for nine months, with courage worthy of the noble man he sought, Stanley pushed on into the interior." Then, 236 days after Stanley reached what is now Tanzania, the most moving meeting in all of missionary history took place. On November 3, 1871, four of the most famous words of the Victorian Era were uttered. Here is the wonderful scene, as related by O. K. Armstrong:

> On November 10 the people of Ugigi rushed to Livingstone to tell him the exciting news: a white man had arrived! Livingstone, emaciated but erect, stood before his tent, peering in astonishment at the big caravan headed by a tall white man flanked by a porter carrying the Stars and Stripes. The people parted to form a living avenue, down

which Stanley stalked to one of the most dramatic meetings of all time.

"Dr. Livingstone, I Presume?"

Stanley came just in time. For two years Livingstone
had been without medicine of any kind. Gratefully he
accepted the new clothes and supplies, eagerly read letters
and heard news of the outside world.

Stanley was never the same man after those days with
Livingstone. His life was completely changed as he witnessed the
faith, courage, and determination of this great man. He pleaded
with Livingstone to return with him to England; but Livingstone
refused, saying, "I still have much work to do." Reluctantly, Stanley
left the lonely explorer and returned with reports for his newspa-
per that made David Livingstone a hero and the most talked-of
man of his day. But fame had little attraction to this courageous
man who gave his life for Africa.

His Prolific Honors

When he returned to England for his first furlough and to
write about his missionary travels, Livingstone was astonished to
find himself famous. He was received at the palace by the prince
consort. Scientists were eager to hear him, and the government gave
him civil authority to deal with African tribes. Manifold honors
were heaped upon him for his work. Altogether he received some
507 medals, freedoms, degrees, and awards. Yet, as one speaker
said at a banquet in Livingstone's honor, "Notwithstanding eighteen months of laudation, so justly bestowed on him by all classes
of his countrymen, and after receiving all the honors which the
universities and cities of our country could shower upon him, he is
still the same honest, true-hearted David Livingstone as when he
issued from the wilds of Africa."

Amid all the adulation coming his way, however, there was a dark cloud that humbled him. To a friend, he wrote, "My son, Robert, is in the Federal Army in America, and no comfort. The secret ballast is often applied by a kind hand above, when to outsiders we appear to be sailing gloriously with the wind."

THE SLAVE EMANCIPATOR

Livingstone not only expanded the geographical knowledge of Central Africa through his explorations, healed the sick, and preached the gospel to the poor; he also fought most relentlessly against the Arab slave trade, which destroyed potential village preaching centers, as a means to promote missionary effort. This unholy, inhuman trafficking was strongly denounced by this fearless emancipator, who wrote fervent letters to the British government begging them to help stop such a terrible trade. Abraham Lincoln and David Livingstone were both lovers of freedom and haters of slavery. Of the latter, it is said, "For thirty years his life was spent in an unwearied effort to evangelize the native races, to explore the undiscovered secrets, and abolish the desolating trade of Central Africa." There are those who set themselves to evangelize, others to explore, and still others to emancipate. But, as Frank Boreham expressed it, "David Livingstone, with a golden secret locked up in his heart, undertook all three. *Evangelization, exploration, emancipation*—these were his watchwords."

Livingstone was haunted by the specter of the slave traffic. The last words he wrote before his death, which are inscribed on his grave in Westminster Abbey as his epitaph for thousands to read, are these:

> All I can say in my solitude is, may Heaven's rich blessing come down on every one—American, English, Turk— who will help to heal this open sore of the World.

At another time, he wrote, "Can the love of Christ not carry the missionary where the slave-trade carries the trader?" His testimony was clear and emphatic wherever slavery prevailed. Neither personal friendship nor any other consideration under the sun could repress his denunciations. He lived in order to free unhappy souls. As J. D. Jones wrote of his master passion,

> Better than all his discoveries would be the healing of this open sore. He tracked the traders to their hunting grounds. He laid bare their unspeakable cruelties. He stirred up the consciences of the people at home. He fought the fight almost single-handed. He surrendered home and comfort, he endured loneliness and suffering: he risked health and life in this holy war, and at last he died, and by dying won his triumph. Other travelers may have made greater discoveries than Livingstone but no one can rob him of this title to immortal fame—*he was the Liberator of Africa!*

His implicit and simple trust in God was the anchor of his soul amid all his toils, trials, and tribulations. He had a profound belief in the power of prayer, and his prayers were direct and plain. Once, when surrounded by savages, he sensed danger in the air but looked to Christ and rested upon His promise: "I read that Jesus said, *'All power is given unto me in heaven and in earth. Go ye therefore, and teach all nations,…and, lo, I am with you alway, even unto the end of the world'* (Matthew 28:18–20). It is the word of a Gentleman of the most sacred and strictest honor, and there is an end on't."

HIS LONELY DEATH

After Stanley had left him, Livingstone, determined explorer that he was, took advantage of his new caravan and restocked supplies and went on in the search for the sources of the Nile. His strength was ebbing, yet he stubbornly continued, and when he was too weak to walk, he was carried on a litter. As he entered further into the interior, he looked around him for a suitable grave. Although he underwent several physical agonies, he was reluctant to give up. Six weeks before he died, he wrote, "Nothing will make me give up my work in despair. I encourage myself in the Lord my God and go forward." The loss of his much-valued medicine chest was the beginning of the end, for after January 1867, he had no remedy against African fevers and other grievous maladies. He described his poignant loss thusly: "I felt as if I had now received the sentence of death: this loss of the medicine gnaws at the heart terribly." What a pitiable sight he must have presented, far in the lonely interior of Africa, in pain and sickness with neither wife nor child nor brother to cheer him with sympathy or lighten his dull, drab hut with a smile! Such was the heavy price he paid to make Christ known in a heathen land.

The solemn end of this warrior has been told over and over again, and it cannot be repeated too often for the inspiration of the young. April 29, 1873, was the last day of his missionary travels. He directed Susi, his faithful servant, to take him to Ilala and lay him on a rough bed in a hut. At four o'clock the next morning, his servants saw the light of a candle burning, but David Livingstone was not in his crude bed. He was kneeling beside his bed with his head resting on his clasped hands—dead. Somehow he had crawled out and, doubtless knowing that the end was at hand, had died in the act of prayer, interceding for his loved ones and his own dear Africa, with all her sins and wrongs. Thus, on May 4, 1873, at sixty years of age, he entered the presence of the King, to be reunited with his beloved Mary and his dear, godly parents. For this gallant saint, there was no moaning at the bar as he put out to sea to explore the heavenly land.

From *but* to hut, village to village, the sad announcement was relayed: "The Good One is gone!" Crowds of his converts came to pay their last respects to the one who had brought them life, light, and hope. The people nearest him knew that those in England who loved and honored him wanted to bury the missionary-doctor, and so with loving hearts they dried and embalmed his frail frame and covered it with bark. Before doing so, however, they removed his heart and buried it beneath a moula tree—a symbolic act, for his heart belonged to their soil. "Africa" was engraved on that heart, the life's blood of which was poured out for its salvation.

Then began the longest, most perilous funeral march in history. The native mourners set out on their nine-month trek to the coast, singing the gospel hymns "The Good One" had taught them. A British vessel at Zanzibar brought the body home to England, arriving on April 15, 1874. On April 18, the famous Scot was laid to rest in honor in Westminster Abbey, where a vast throng had gathered to pay their last respects. Perhaps one of the most intimate and inspiring biographies of this missionary-explorer is *The Personal Life of David Livingstone* by W. G. Blaikie, whose very good summary of his worth and witness we quote:

> Amid all the vicissitudes of his career, Livingstone remained faithful to his missionary character. His warmth and purity of heart, his intense devotion to his Master, and the African people for his Master's sake, his patience, endurance, trustfulness, and prayerfulness, his love of science, his wide humanity, his intense charity, have given to his name and memory an undying fragrance. After his death, church after church hastened to send missionaries to Africa; and it would take a long space even to enumerate all the agencies that are at work there. His death, that seemed to give the death-blow to his plans, gave a new impulse to the cause of African evangelization and civilization, which bids fair, with God's help, to accomplish great results.

Although Livingstone did not live to see the cessation of the slavery he utterly abhorred and fought so hard to abolish, after his death, Queen Victoria publicly acclaimed the missionary for his unceasing crusade against this horror, and in 1880, she announced that treaties had been signed with the sultan of Zanzibar and other sovereigns prohibiting this terrible traffic by land and sea.

What are some of the lessons to be gleaned today from the noble life and magnificent labors of this renowned medical missionary, who suffered and yet achieved so much for the Master he dearly loved and faithfully served?

Give the Best to God

From his deathbed, David Hogg, his old Sunday school teacher, gave young Livingstone the instruction, "Now, lad, make religion the everyday business of your life and not a thing of fits and starts; for if you do, temptation and other things will get the better of you." From first to last, David Livingstone made religion—or, rather, Christ and His cause—his everyday business. As his *Journal* records, on his last birthday he dedicated himself anew to Him to whom he had surrendered his life. If Christ is worthy of anything, it is our best, seeing that He shed His blood for our redemption. Calvary has a claim upon all that we are and have.

> Just as I am, young, strong, and free,
> To be the best that I can be,
> For truth, and righteousness, and Thee,
> Lord of my life, I come.[7]

Reliance upon Divine Companionship

With all his heart, Livingstone believed the Master's promise to accompany without fail those He would send forth into all the world to extend His cause among men. When home on furlough

---

7. Marianne Hearn, "Just As I Am, Thine Own to Be," 1887.

after years of service in Africa, Livingstone went to his old university in Glasgow to receive the degree Doctor of Laws. As he rose, he was not met with student banter. His gaunt, haggard frame, the result of his long exposure to the African sun, was received in reverential silence. Already he had on thirty occasions suffered fevers and severe illnesses. His crushed arm, the result of his encounter with the lion, was hanging at his side. Replying to the honor conferred upon him, he said, "I return to my work without misgiving and with great gladness. Would you like me to tell you what supported me through all the years of exile among people whose language I could not understand, and whose attitude towards me was always uncertain and often hostile? It was this: *'Lo, I am with you always, even unto the end of the world'* (Matthew 28:20). On those words I staked everything, and they never failed."

Livingstone proved that with the "*Go*," there was the "*Lo*"— that whomever God appoints for soul-saving service, He accompanies. Is it not said of the disciples after Jesus had ascended to heaven that as they went forth preaching everywhere, and that the Lord worked *with them* and confirmed their witness? (See Mark 16:20.) Facing the unknown, Moses received the divine promise *"My presence shall go with thee"* (Exodus 33:14). Without divine companionship, the leader of the people would not go forward: *"If thy presence go not with me, carry us not up hence"* (verses 14–15). Whether we are called to follow Livingstone into the regions beyond or to tarry by the staff at home makes no difference. All followers of the Master have the assurance that He will never leave them nor forsake them.

> Wherever He may guide me,
> No want shall turn me back;
> My Shepherd is beside me,
> And nothing can I lack.
> His wisdom ever waketh,
> His sight is never dim;

He knows the way He taketh,
And I will walk with Him.[8]

Live the Life That Counts

After visiting Cambridge to address the university students, Livingstone received a most encouraging letter from one of the tutors, part of which read, "That Cambridge visit of yours lighted a candle which will never, never go out." Such a sentiment is true of the renowned missionary's work in Africa. His light continued to shine until extinguished by his lonely death, and the influence of his wonderful labors continues. Florence Nightingale wrote to Livingstone's sister after hearing of his death in Africa and said, "He has opened those countries for God to enter in. He struck the first blow to abolish a hideous slave trade. He, like Stephen, was the first martyr."

Although his heart is buried under an African tree and his body reposes in Westminster Abbey, his spirit goes marching on. The history of his life was not completed with the record of his death. Africa is a different continent today because of Livingstone's sacrifice on its behalf. Do you remember the appealing lines of Rudyard Kipling's poem "If"?

If you can talk with crowds and keep your virtue,
Or walk with Kings—nor lose the common touch,
If neither foes nor loving friends can hurt you,
If all men count with you, but none too much;
If you can fill the unforgiving minute
With sixty seconds' worth of distance run,
Yours is the Earth and everything that's in it,
And—which is more—you'll be a Man, my son.

The thrilling biography of David Livingstone proves that he was such a man. For over thirty years, he lived life to its limit and

8. Anna L. Waring, "In Heavenly Love Abiding," 1850.

gave until he could give no more for the soul of Africa. The story is told of a man in a Scottish prison who had been a fellow Sunday school scholar in Livingstone's youth and who was deeply moved when he heard of Livingstone's burial in Westminster Abbey. What a contrast in the use of life! The one lad went forth to make his life count for Christ, but the other lad made his life count for crime. If we

> Live for Christ, we live again,
> Live for self, we live in vain.

CHAPTER 6

JOHN BUNYAN: THE FAMOUS TINKER OF BEDFORD

No book except the Bible has been translated into as many languages as *The Pilgrim's Progress* by John Bunyan, yet it is to be regretted that what used to be a household name means very little today to many young people—and older people, too, for that matter. For centuries, not only the names but also the subjects in that volume were sources of great spiritual instruction and profit. To countless numbers now "high in bliss upon the hills of God," Bunyan's *Pilgrim's Progress* first set "the joy-bells ringing in the City of Habitation."

There are those who argue that since *The Pilgrim's Progress* has always been such a popular book, and since Bunyan is such a famous man in English history, that any explanatory word about the man and his works is quite superfluous. But while the majority of Christian people may possess a copy of Bunyan's masterpiece, yet the author and his works are practically unknown by today's young people. Perhaps they are neglected because, compared with the light, popular literature of contemporary society, books like *The Pilgrim's Progress* and *The Holy War* make for hard and dry reading to all, save for devout and diligent Bible students. Thus a shallow, superficial knowledge of the Bedford tinker satisfies the majority of young people, even in religious circles.

In his *Ten Bunyan Talks*, G. W. MacGown speaks of a twenty-three-year-old-daughter of a minister who had been to both private and boarding schools and was asked if she knew who John Bunyan was. "Oh, he wrote *Paradise Lost* and was born blind," she replied. The poor girl had him confused with John Milton. Evidently she had not spent much time in Bunyan's company. Had she done so, she would have found it to yield fruit a hundredfold for the strengthening and stimulating of her spiritual being.

When I preached in Bedford several years ago, I remember how I stood in awe before Bunyan's magnificent monument, reposing where four roads meet in the heart of the city. In 1874, the Duke of Bedford, a descendant of Lord William Russell, the martyr to liberty, presented this most costly and beautiful statue of Bunyan to the city, in Bunyan's memory. The unveiling occurred on June 10, 1874, one of the greatest days Bedford had ever known. Thousands of distinguished persons from all over the country assembled for the unveiling, which was performed by Lady Augusta Stanley, sister of the Earl of Elgin and wife of Dean Stanley of Westminster.

The statue itself is bronze, cast of cannons and bells brought from China, weighing two-and-a-half tons. The figure of Bunyan, cast from a portrait of him painted by Sadler, is ten feet high. The sculptor, Boehm, tried to present the inscription on the pedestal of "a very grave person," and he succeeded admirably. There Bunyan in bronze has stood for one hundred years now, "as if he pleaded with men." The entire press of the time in laudatory articles on the "Tinker of Bedford" called him blessed among men.

The immense crowds assembled on that historic day were addressed by several conspicuous persons, including Dean Stanley, who concluded his eulogy by saying, "Let everyone of you who has not read *The Pilgrim's Progress*—if there be any such person—read it without delay. Let those who have read it a hundred times read it again for the hundred and first time; and then follow out in your lives the lessons it teaches. You will then all be better monuments of John Bunyan than even this magnificent statue."

The England of Bunyan's period, from 1628 to 1688, embraces one of the most stirring in English history. Dr. George Cheever, in his lectures on "Bunyan," tells us that "it was an age of great revolutions, great excitement, great genius, great talents, great extremes in both good and evil, great piety and great wickedness, great freedom and great tyranny and oppression. Under Cromwell there was great liberty and prosperity; under the Charleses there was great oppression and disgrace." Charles II, whose reign was one of tyranny, was among the most dissolute, worthless, corrupt kings who ever sat on England's throne.

Yet, in the midst of such darkness, there were those who remained true to God's cause. In spite of the passing of hard measures like the Corporation Act, concocted for the destruction of religious liberty, there were men willing to endure hardship and sacrifice for Christ's sake. In eminent saints like Baster, Owen, Howe, Goodwin, and others, who were contemporaries of Bunyan, we have a few pearls sunk in deep and troubled mire, out of which they were to be taken and placed in a more glorious setting.

BUNYAN'S BACKGROUND

Bunyan himself was born in the village of Elstow, about a mile from Bedford, in November 1628. His father was a brazier—that is, a mender of pots, pans, and kettles—as was this writer's father for over sixty years. In common with the majority of workers in tin who did not carry on their trades all the year round at the same bench, Bunyan Senior was dubbed a tinker and was considered by some to be of Gypsy descent. The records of his family are traceable to about A.D. 1200, and the name, then known as *Buignon*, indicates that the family was of Norman origin. As the great descendant of such an ancient house, Bunyan, by his life and work, brought much credit upon it. One of his contemporaries described him as being "tall of stature, strong-browed, with sparkling eyes, wearing hair on his lip after the old British fashion; his hair was reddish, but in his latter days sprinkled with gray; his nose well cut, his mouth moderately large, his forehead something high, and his habit [dress] always plain and modest."

In his matchless *Grace Abounding*, Bunyan's autobiography, he reveals his own lowly parentage and descent, of which he was unashamed:

> For my descent then, it was, as is well known by many, of a low and inconsiderable generation; my father's house being of that rank that is meanest, and most despised of all the families in the land.

It would seem that Bunyan learned much about the work of a brazier, for, after his marriage and conversion, he worked for five or six years at the trade in order to support his family. He wandered from village to village as a tinker, his swarthy face made swarthier yet by the smoke of his pitch kettle. The outstanding facts of Bunyan's early life prove how the Divine Potter was at work, shaping His honorable vessel.

As to his education, Bunyan was not a child of the university. He attended a Bedford school for the poor. There was no compulsory education in his day; legal enforcement would have been laughed at then. While an apt pupil, he must have quickly lost all he had learned. "I confess I did soon lose that little I learned, and that almost utterly," he confessed. One of the expositors of *The Pilgrim's Progress* remarks that such a classic could not have had so much of its beauty or truth if Bunyan's soul had been steeped in scholastic discipline. He was divinely taught. Under the schooling of the Holy Spirit, unaided by acquired wisdom, he produced one of the greatest literary masterpieces in the world.

Bunyan's boyhood years were reckless and profane. He narrowly escaped death when he fell from a boat in the River Ouse. This experience had a good effect on him for the time being, but he soon lost his contrition and gratitude in further prodigality. In those sinful years of his youth, he had dreams full of horror because of terrible judgments hanging over his guilty head. His mind was haunted by visions of deserved punishment at the hands of a despised and insulted God.

He appears to have developed in early years a headstrong disposition that often led him into youthful excesses. But his youth was not particularly loose or disreputable. His own harsh self-accusations were the severe judgment of a heart and conscience keenly alive to a sense of sin. We may be inclined to feel that he was apt to overdo his expression of self-defamation. But, as G. W. MacGown expresses it, "Such strong denunciations must be taken as the exaggeration of a highly strung and sensitive moral nature in revolt against its former lawless and reckless self."

Yet, even in those tender years, Bunyan was notorious for his command of language—of a lurid sort—and for his power of storytelling, especially when he wanted to get out of a difficult situation. What a master of the rich Anglo-Saxon tongue he became!

Something must be said about the military career of this young man, who had few equals in swearing and who gathered fame as a ringleader in all manner of vice and ungodliness. Around 1645, Bunyan enlisted in the Parliamentary Army and took part in the siege of Leicester. During his military career, he had another providential escape from death, which made a deep impression on his wicked mind. He was drawn by lot to be one of the besiegers, but just as he was ready to go out on the perilous mission, another soldier desired to substitute for him. "To which," says Bunyan, "when I had consented, he took my place; and coming to the siege, as he stood sentinel, he was shot in the head with a musket bullet, and died." Unhappily, the impression soon faded, as Bunyan's own confession states: "Here were judgments and mercy, but neither of them did awaken my soul to righteousness; whereof I sinned still, and grew more and more rebellious against God, and careless of my own salvation."

HIS CONVERSION AND SUBSEQUENT CAREER

Bunyan was converted through an experience that had its Slough of Despond and its Valley of the Shadow of Death, of which he was to write so vividly. One day, he overheard the talk or gossip of three godly women as they exchanged thoughts about holy things and the state of their souls "as if joy did make them speak." "This was indeed true gossip—God-sib—conversation that showed the relationship of God to human souls." Bunyan's heart tarried with the female trio as they spoke, and true conviction set itself firmly in his heart. Through the influence of these good women, he was introduced to the Baptist minister of the town, John Gifford, a stalwart Christian whose godly life and teaching did much to set Bunyan up as a staunch and valiant soldier of the cross. He was baptized in 1653 and very soon after entered the Baptist ministry.

At twenty-eight years of age, he ventured to preach, and he began by telling others of his own strange journey from the City of Destruction to the cross, where his burden had fallen off and he'd been freed. With a growing passion to preach, he evangelized the countryside around his home. Crowds gathered to listen to the man they had learned to revere as "Bishop Bunyan." One of his contemporaries wrote, "I have seen about 1200; and I computed about 3,000 that came to hear him on a Lord's Day, so that a half of them were obliged to return for want of room. He had an intense love for souls, and an absolute faith in the power of the Gospel to save all who would believe."

As he progressed in his preaching, he developed an incomparable style and came to use the noblest and purest Saxon ever used in the pulpit. He had an imagination that places him beside Dante, the greatest poet of the dead, and the blind John Milton. He won the hearts of all by "his homely humor, charmed with his shrewd mother-wit, and touched with his wise and hospitable sympathy."

Another significant episode in his life was his marriage at the age of twenty. When the Parliamentary Army was disbanded, Bunyan returned to Elstow and in 1649 set himself up as a tinker, trundling his machine from village to village. The sweet young girl he married brought him no dowry of worldly wealth. "She was virtuous, loving, born of good, honest and godly parents who had instructed her as well as they were able in the ways of truth and saving knowledge."

The young wife's only dowry consisted of two pious books brought from her home—*The Plain Man's Pathway to Heaven* by Bishop Baily and *Practice of Piety* by Arthur Kent. Bunyan read these books with his wife and was greatly influenced by them. His *Life and Death of Mr. Badman*, published in 1680, somewhat resembles the truth gleaned from these two books, which God used to awaken desires for a new life in Bunyan. Now he started attending church and reading religious books with more enthusiasm. He found delight in the Bible, and no storm-tossed mariner upon an unknown sea could have pored over his chart with greaer eagerness. These two small volumes served to deepen the conviction of spiritual need that had already brought the young tinker into great trouble and depression of mind. Through the reading of these books, Bunyan gave up worldly amusements and set out to live a life of strict and austere conflict. Reformation had started, and it finally led to peace of heart in believing on Christ.

After nine or ten years of wedded bliss, Bunyan's wife, who had enlivened the home with six children, passed away. In 1659, Bunyan remarried, principally because he was often away preaching and needed someone to care for his home and children, especially his beloved blind daughter, Mary. He was happy in his choice of a second wife, a noble woman who earnestly pled her husband's cause before Judge Hales after he had spent a year in prison. Dr. Cheever says of this court case, "The scene is worthy of the pencil of some great painter when, without a creature to befriend or sustain her, this young and trembling woman, unaccustomed to and abashed at such presences, entered the courtroom and stood before the judges, in the midst of the crowd of justices and gentry of the country assembled." Truly she was a partaker of her husband's own spirit, a heroine of no ordinary stamp. Her advocacy, however, was of no avail. Bunyan spent twelve full years in prison, all because he refused to discontinue public preaching. While in prison, he was allowed to make bootlaces, which enabled him to contribute to the support of his family.

HIS ACHIEVEMENTS WHILE INCARCERATED

It was during the dark days of the persecution of the Nonconformists in England that Bunyan was thrown into prison, and he preached to all who could gain access to him. The story runs that his prison keeper had such confidence in Bunyan's honesty that he would often let him out to meet his congregation in the half-hidden dells and retired woods, where he could minister to them disguised as a carter, while scouts on the outskirts of the crowds kept watch against intruders.

The magistrates offered him his liberty if he would refrain from preaching, but he scorned the offer, saying, "If you let me out today, I should preach tomorrow." He could not be silent, for he had a passion to preach what he himself had tasted and handled of the Word of Life. The visits of his wife and children make for sorrowful reading. Parting with them was like "cutting the flesh from my bones," Bunyan would say. Under the Declaration of Indulgence granted by Charles II, Bunyan was released. His prison days were ruled by God, however, and out of them came the first part of *The Pilgrim's Progress.*

As a writer of allegory, Bunyan has never been excelled. Our admiration for him increases as we remember that although he lived in an age of unparalleled literary profligacy, there is neither a line in his writings nor a word in his sermons that can be charged with coarseness. English literature of his day had become thoroughly imbued with all the elements of poetry, fiction, and romance. Saxon English was "prepared to his hand; being full of image and awe, of wonder and grandeur, which he could express to the popular mind in a very racy style. Unconsciously he felt the force of his mother tongue; it stimulated his genius, became the groundwork of his thought and the model of his utterance; a choice which places him side by side with Shakespeare and the English Bible as one of the great conservators of our powerful language."

Macaulay's estimation of him as a writer and a preacher is true: "No writer has said more exactly what he meant to say. For magnificence, for pathos, for vehement exhortation, for subtle disquisition, for every purpose of the poet and orator and the divine, the homely dialect is perfectly sufficient. No book shows so well as does *Pilgrim's Progress* how rich our language is in its own proper wealth, and how little it has improved by all it has borrowed."

Matthew Arnold wrote in his *Mixed Essays,*

We have the Philistine of genius in Religion—Luther.
We have the Philistine of genius in Politics—Cromwell.
We have the Philistine of genius in Literature—Bunyan.

Bunyan's pen was always busy. Altogether some sixty works flowed from it. His publisher added this quaint note to his literary productions: "Here are 60 pieces of his works, and he was 60 years of age." None of his many books, however, bears comparison with *The Pilgrim's Progress*. Untold thousands of copies of this book have been published since he wrote it in prison. In Lennox Library, New York, can be found the most extensive collection in existence. Some three hundred editions of the work in English and seventy-four in different foreign languages are housed there. It passed through eight editions in the first thirty years of its pilgrimage. In fact, no book has been rendered into so many editions and languages except the Bible itself. *The Pilgrim's Progress* has always been the delight of the lowly, and it has exerted a fascinating power on the most cultured and gifted minds. It ranks among the masterpieces of English literature, and eternity alone will reveal the blessing it has been to multitudes in finding Christ as the Way, the Truth, and the Life. It has intrinsic worth as an inexhaustible mine of Christian stimulus and example.

The Pilgrim's Progress takes its place among the transcendently great works of English literature, as testified to by many outstanding writers. J. R. Green, for instance, in his remarkable *Short History of the English People*, says of it:

> In its range, its directness, in its simple grace, in the ease with which it changes from lively dialogue to dramatic action, from simple pathos to passionate earnestness, in the subtle and delicate fancy which often suffuses its child-like words, in its playful humor, its bold character painting, in the even and balanced power which passes without effort from the Valley of the Shadow of Death to the land "where the Shining Ones commonly walked because the border of Heaven," in its sunny kindliness, unbroken by one bitter word, *The Pilgrim's Progress* is amongst the noblest of English poems. For if Puritanism

had first discovered the poetry which contact with the spiritual world awakes in the meanest souls, Bunyan was the first of the Puritans who revealed this.

This is indeed high yet worthy praise, and many others have affirmed it. Dr. Samuel Johnson said that *The Pilgrim's Progress* was one of two or three works that he wished were longer. "He praised John Bunyan highly," wrote Boswell in his *Life of Johnson*, "and said that *The Pilgrim's Progress* had great merit both for invention and imagination, and the conduct of the story, and it had the best evidence of its merit, the general and continued approbation of mankind."

Robert Louis Stevenson was another who lauded the worth of this great work of Bunyan's. Writing on books that had influenced him, he said, "Lastly, I must name *The Pilgrim's Progress*, a book that breathes of every beautiful and valuable emotion." Dr. John Kelmen, who himself wrote an appealing appraisal of Bunyan and his word, said of Stevenson that "*The Pilgrim's Progress* was the book in all English literature which he knew best, and to which he oftenest alluded."

While it ranks among the most original of English works of genius, there is actually no book so little original or so dependent throughout on a higher source. As to Bunyan's terse English, doubtless he learned it from Spenser and Chaucer; of human nature, he borrowed from himself and his circumstances; of history, he gathered much from Foxe's *Book of Martyrs*; of hallowed conviction, he caught from the Holy Spirit; and of uncrippled boldness, this was inspired by his love of soul-liberty. But his writings are full of truth because of his daily delight in Bible meditation. Bunyan was the man "with a Book in his hand," and Scripture was the source of his unique, incomparable literary style. His entire dependence upon "the best of books" made him the creative genius he was. J. R. Green says,

The images of *The Pilgrim's Progress* are the images of Prophet and Evangelist; it borrows for its tenderer outbursts the very verse of the Song of Songs, and pictures the Heavenly City in the words of the Apocalypse. But so completely has the Bible become Bunyan's life, that one feels its phrases as the natural expression of his thoughts. He has lived in the Bible till its words have become his own. In no book do we see more clearly the new imaginative force which had been given to the common life of Englishmen by their study of the Bible. Its English is the simplest and homeliest English which has ever been used by any great English writer; but it is the English of the Bible.

Bunyan represents the Bible as having tremendous influence upon Pilgrim, the hero of his story, who "opened the Book and read therein" and broke out with the lamentable cry, "What shall I do?" Later on, we have the phrase "He was, as he was wont, reading in his Book." Coleridge said of *The Pilgrim's Progress* that it was "incomparably the best compendium of Gospel truth ever produced by a writer not miraculously inspired." Macaulay said of another work of Bunyan's—*Grace Abounding*—that it "is indeed one of the most remarkable pieces of autobiography in the world." In this, we have the charming natural account of his own progress in Bible reading. From the time he "began to look into the Bible with new eyes," he found himself held captive by its revelation of what his own soul needed most.

In his monumental volume *The History of Baptists*, in the section devoted to John Bunyan the Baptist preacher of Bedford, Dr. Thomas Armitage reminds us of Dean Stanley's witness to the influence of *The Pilgrim's Progress* on his own life:

When in early life I lighted upon the passage where the Pilgrim is taken into the House Beautiful to see the pedigree of the Ancient of Days, and the varieties and histories of that place, both ancient and modern, I determined that if ever the time should arrive when I should become a Professor of Ecclesiastical History, these should become the opening words in which I would describe the treasures of that magnificent store-house. Accordingly, when, many years after, it so fell out, I could find no better mode of beginning my course at Oxford than by redeeming that early pledge; and when the course came to an end, and I wished to draw a picture of the prospects still reserved for the future of Christendom, I found again the best words I could supply were those in which, on leaving the Beautiful House, Christian was shown in the distance the view of the Delectable Mountains, "which they said would add to his comfort because they were nearer to the desired haven."

Dr. Armitage then observes, "This was a worthy and heartfelt tribute from Westminster to the dreaming tinker whose effigy now adorns the House of Commons, side by side with those of orators, heroes and statesmen in honour of the man, who though he 'devilishly' abstained from attending the church, 'contrary to the laws of the king,' has preached in all pulpits and palaces ever since."

LESSONS FROM HIS LIFE

What are some of the lessons to be gleaned from the sixty years of this Bedford preacher and author who lived while a long list of the most remarkable events in England occurred? First of all, his experience magnifies the grace abounding he wrote so wonderfully about. Too many present-day preachers are either too afraid or too ashamed to preach the glorious evangelical truths Bunyan clothed with such picturesque imagery. Men are lost in sin and are on their way to the City of Destruction, and we fail in our vocation if we do not lead them to the cross, where the burden of sin rolls away. Sin and salvation, heaven and hell, were real to Bunyan, and he was perpetually valiant for these truths.

Then there was his deep and ever-deepening love for the Bible, which to Bunyan was not one of the best but *the* best of books. The Word was part and parcel of his life. After he had been in prison for three months, he was offered his freedom if he would go to some Bedford church to hear the Prayer Book that he detested read. But Bunyan stoutly refused, saying to the clerk of the court who had come with the message of proffered release, "I will stand by the truth to the last drop of my blood." Perhaps the tragic decline in church membership would be arrested if we had more men of this caliber. Bunyan never preached uncertainties but always positive truths.

Further, Bunyan was willing to suffer for the faith. At the beginning of his imprisonment, he expected to suffer martyrdom on the gallows. "This, therefore, lay with great trouble upon me, for methought I was ashamed to die with a false face and tottering knees for such a cause as this"—his hatred for the Prayer Book, which "muzzles up prayer in a form," and which he resisted to the end. Listen to this brave confession of his: "I have determined, the almighty God being my helper and shield, yet to suffer if frail life may continue so long, even till the moss shall grow on mine eyebrows, rather than thus to violate my faith and principles."

Today, many young men leave schools of cultural and theological learning and are pitch-forked into the ministry Bunyan deemed so sacred, with little "faith and principles." We know those who, in their training, gained degrees but lost their convictions and who made it evident in their efforts to preach that they doubted their beliefs and believed their doubts. Would that these messageless preachers would saturate their minds with the sixty volumes of John Bunyan, who stood at all times as if he pleaded with men!

At the early age of six, C. H. Spurgeon, with a passion for books and pictures, delighted in reading *The Pilgrim's Progress* and Bunyan's other works. No wonder he became a prince among preachers!

After Bunyan's release from prison, he became one of the most popular gospel preachers in all the land. People of every rank listened to his impassioned appeals. Charles II asked Dr. John Owen how he, a man of profound learning, could listen to a tinker preach. Dr. Owen replied, "May it please your Majesty, had I the tinker's abilities for preaching, I would gladly relinquish all my learning."

Upon the death of John Gifford, pastor of Bedford Church, Bunyan was called to the oversight of the work and became a much-loved minister of the gospel. The year of the Revolution, 1688, saw the end of his earthly pilgrimage. He died on August 12, 1688, at the age of sixty. One of his last acts was the reconciliation of a father and son who had quarreled. Successful in this blessed act, he returned home in a drenching rain, caught a chill, and died ten days later. His last words were, "Take me, for I come to Thee." He was buried in Bunhill Fields, where his well-kept monument—bearing simply his name—gives inspiration to all visitors of every nationality.

Bunyan's much-loved little blind daughter, Mary, often visited her father in prison and brought him small gifts for his solace. She had great concern for him and often, when parting from him, would put her delicate little fingers to his eyes and cheeks to feel if any tears flowed, that she might kiss them away. This precious, sightless child died and left her father, who treasured her precious memory, in prison. She entered the Celestial Gate first to wait as a "shining one" watching for the coming of her dear father. She did not have to wait long. When Bunyan entered into the Celestial City, he saw not only the King in His beauty but also for the first time saw his Mary's sweet eyes ablaze with light. She did not raise a hand to her valiant father's cheek, as she had at the prison prison, however, for God had wiped away all tears from Bunyan's eyes, even as He had banished blindness from the young pilgrim's eyes. What a meeting that must have been!

On his dying bed, Bunyan acted the part of *Hopeful*, crossing the River of Death. "So he passed over, and all the trumpets sounded for him on the other side."

At last, as Pilgrim himself, Bunyan entered the Celestial City, whose towers glisten with a light fairer than day. Although dead for nearly three centuries, Bunyan still speaks in those monumental writings he left behind, which continue to enrich countless lives.

CHAPTER 7

JOHN WESLEY: THE EVANGELIST WHO PREVENTED A BLOODY REVOLUTION

Lecky, the historian who affirmed that "the conversion of John Wesley formed one of the grand epochs of English history," is the one who tells us that the Methodist revival saved England a terrible revolution, which, at that time, had engulfed France and seemed ready to sweep across the Channel to bring a bloodbath to England. But the mighty spiritual revival under George Whitefield and the Wesleys caused the tide to turn through the remarkable outburst of practical Christianity. More than any other man since that sixteenth century, John Wesley stands out as the most outstanding religious leader who influenced the masses for God and righteousness.

John Wesley was born in one of the darkest periods of English history. Appalling conditions made the country ripe for a revolution. There was the iniquitous slave traffic. Prisons were dens of cruelty and the foulest immorality, from which prisoners could escape only by starvation or by jail fever that festered without ceasing in those haunts of human wretchedness. Purity and fidelity to the marriage vow were sneered at, considered out of fashion. Schools were scarce, crowds of children being denied moral or religious training of any sort. Mobs rioted, burned houses, flung open prisons, and robbed homes and ships at will. Ruthless laws, like the one that ruled a person should be hanged for cutting down a tree or for thieving, only caused the criminal class to become more bold and prolific. In higher circles, anyone who talked of religion was laughed at.

Hannah More, the English religious writer and reformer, reported, "We saw but one Bible in the parish of Cheddar and that was used to prop up a flowerpot." Drunkenness also prevailed, for people could get drunk for a penny. It was a time of open profanity. "The Blasters Club," made up of youths who professed to be servants of the devil, came together to offer prayers in his name. Such utter disregard for sacred things had never been known in England before. At one time, Wesley visited the low quarter of Newcastle-upon-Tyne, where he stood by the old pump and preached the gospel. His text was Isaiah 53:5: *"He was wounded for our transgressions, he was bruised for our iniquities."* One who was present said afterward that "Wesley's tenderness was such that these poor and wicked people clung to his hands and his clothes when he had finished." But Wesley himself said of the crowd, "Such blasphemy, such cursing, such swearing, even from the mouths of little children! Surely this place is ripe for the Master."

Such were the bad old days Wesley was born in, and God made him the channel of a spiritual revolution that helped to change society, the fruit of which abides in religious and philanthropic agencies. As Woodrow Wilson, twenty-eighth president of the United States (1913–1921), wrote, "The 18th century cried out for deliverance and light, and God prepared John Wesley to show the world the might and blessing of His salvation." As we think of the corrupt, violent forces at work today, well might we pray for another mighty movement of the Spirit of God such as England experienced at the beginning of the eighteenth century. We thus come to look at the portrait of England's never-to-be-forgotten evangelist of the highways and byways.

HIS GODLY HERITAGE

Behind John Wesley was a godly ancestry that helped to mold him into the potent influence he became. His pedigree proves that God was preparing him to come to the kingdom at the time he did.

His great-grandfather was Bartholomew Wesley, a Puritan of renown and a great stalwart for the truth during the reign of Charles II.

His grandfather was John Wesley, Bartholomew's son, who for a time acted as a minister at Poole. (The John Wesley we are considering was named after him.) Thus, as one historian expresses it, "As far as we can trace them back, we find Wesley's ancestors respectable for learning, conspicuous for piety, and firmly attached to those new views of Christianity which they had learned from Scripture."

His father was Samuel Wesley, who was born in November 1662 in Dorset and died in 1735 at Epworth. While his early life was spent among the Dissenters, he came to associate himself with the Church of England in 1685. After graduating from Oxford in 1688, he served several churches but ultimately settled down in Epworth, Lincolnshire. His salary was paid by Queen Mary in 1696 in recognition of his dedication of his *Life in Christ: An Heroic Poem*. A versatile writer, both in prose and verse, he was able to eke out his salary by his pen. He wrote several hymns, among them "Behold the Saviour of Mankind." He also penned an exposition on the book of Job. For some forty years, he struggled against poverty, yet he toiled on in obscurity and penury and became the father of the great Apostle of Methodism.

Wesley's mother was Susannah, born January 1669 in London; she died there in July 1742. Her father was Samuel Annesley, L.L.D., an eminent Nonconformist minister. At the age of thirteen, Susannah united with the Church of England. She was twenty when she married Samuel Wesley in 1689. She became the mother of nineteen children, nine of whom died in infancy. The story of her home life, the training of her children, and the beauty and devotion of her Christian character reveal her to have been a remarkable woman. Herself one of twenty-five children born to her parents, she knew all about the young. She educated her children herself, and although she subdued their wills, she did not forfeit their affection. John Wesley based an idealized picture of women on her that in later years frustrated his own dreams of a happy marriage and family life. Adam Clarke, the renowned expositor, wrote of her, "Many daughters have done virtuously but Susannah Wesley has excelled them all." Although her family was so numerous, yet she had time for each child. Each night she would take one aside for instruction in divine things. John, the second son, born on June 17, 1703, was nurtured in this way, and in later life he wrote of her he revered thusly: "I cannot remember ever having kept back a doubt from my mother. She was the one heart to whom I went in absolute confidence from my babyhood until the day of her death."

In the day of his great power, Napoleon said, "The greatest need of France is mothers." Our generation desperately needs godly mothers and homes in which spiritual giants like Charles and John Wesley can be reared. When he was only six years of age, John nearly lost his life through the burning of the parsonage, which was set on fire, according to his own account, by some of the angry parishioners who resented his dear father's plain preaching. The fire always remained vivid in his memory, and he mentioned it frequently in his writings. He described himself as "a brand plucked out of the burning." His musically gifted brother Charles might have spiritualized this same incident when he wrote,

> Where shall my wond'ring soul begin?
> How shall I all to Heaven aspire?
> A slave redeem'd from death and sin,
> A brand pluck'd from eternal fire.[9]

THE SCHOLASTIC CAREER

At the early age of six, John Wesley was sent to the Charterhouse School, London, where he stayed for six years. It was there that he cast off some of the home restraints. Commenting on his sojourn at this renowned school, he said, "I entered it a saint and left it a sinner." Maintaining a semblance of outward goodness, he hoped to be saved, as he expressed it, by

> Not being as bad as other people.
> Having still a kindness for Religion.
> Reading the Bible, saying my prayers, going to church.

During his first years at Charterhouse, he had to endure a good deal of bullying from the older boys who used to eat his meat and leave him nothing but a piece of bread for a meal. But he was hardy, and he obeyed his father's strict command to run around the school grounds three times every morning. He remained affectionately attached to Charterhouse and visited it yearly until the end of his life. While a resident there, he became a diligent and clever scholar and even taught Greek before he left.

In 1720, Wesley went to Christ Church, Oxford, where he distinguished himself. During his second year there, he began to plan his studies more carefully with a view of the future. He wrote grammars in five languages and for years was a Fellow of Oxford.

---

9. Charles Wesley, "Where Shall My Wandering Soul Begin?"

After his graduation in 1724, encouraged by his godly parents, he resolved to take Holy Orders, and for two years he assisted his father as curate at Epworth. In 1725, he was made a deacon by the bishop of Oxford, and in 1726 he was elected a Fellow of Lincoln College. In 1728, he was ordained a priest. In spite of his pronounced academic leanings and strong religious background, his religion was all of works. He seemed to be groping in darkness and yearning for the true light.

In 1729, when Wesley was recalled to Oxford to fulfill the residential conditions of his Fellowship, another milestone was reached in his spiritual pilgrimage. Returning, he found his brother Charles, an undergraduate who was to become the Poet of Methodism, joined with Robert and William Morgan in regular studies and devotions. John Wesley immediately joined up with them, and Charles handed the leadership of this religious study circle over to him. The group grew in numbers and influence, even as it earned many nicknames from less religious students. George Whitefield, who became Orpheus of the pulpit and one of the greatest of revival orators, was also closely identified with the circle.

Because these young men observed strictly their self-imposed religious ways, they became known as "The Holy Club." They would read divinity on Sunday evenings and the classics on other days, along with Greek Testament readings. When possible, they would visit the prisons and also the ailing poor of the town. John Wesley once said, "We were now about fifteen in number, all of one heart and of one mind." The nickname "Methodist" was coined because of the methodical way these students lived. They were unusually precise, strict, and methodical in the observance of their religious duties and in the regularity of their lives, rising at four every morning for prayer and devotion. And so, although this nickname was tauntingly given, it actually described their belief that "order is heaven's first law." As the club grew, social service became an important emphasis among its activities. They taught prisoners to read and write and helped them to find work when they were released. They visited workhouses and the homes of the very poor and distributed food, clothes, medicine, and books among the needy. Members of the club also ran a school.

HIS CHURCH AFFILIATION

Although Wesley became the founder of one of the largest Nonconformist denominations in Christendom, he himself never ceased to be a Church of England minister. At one point, he declared, "I affirm once more I live and die a member of the Church of England and that none who regard my advice will ever separate from it." It was his father's wish that he should succeed him as minister at Epworth, but he was so wedded to college life and to his chosen companions that he could not be persuaded to consent, even though he loved the Anglican Church. To the last, Wesley clung passionately to that church and looked on the large body of followers he had gathered as but a lay society in full communion with the church he considered himself a part of.

The reason he broke with the Moravians, who were his earliest friends in the new movement he founded, was because of their contempt for the religious forms of the Church of England. When he became convinced that his life's work was the proclamation of the good news of salvation by faith, he felt that he was recalling his church to its spiritual mission and therefore had no thought of creating a new ecclesiastical organization. All he wanted to do was to make others sharers of his own newfound spiritual riches. The world he lived in was weary of apologies for Christianity. What it needed was the declaration of the love of God for sinners—and Wesley became a herald of such a message.

John Wesley, an Arminian, parted with his impulsive friend Whitefield because of his extravagant Calvinism. Yet this untiring evangelist was extremely tolerant. In fact, it has been said that no other Reformer whom the world has ever seen "so united faithful-ness to the essential doctrines of revelation with charity towards men of every church and creed." When rebuked by the bishop of Lincoln for his recognition of other church bodies, Wesley replied, "Alas! My lord, is this a time to persecute any man for conscience sake? I beseech you do as you would be done by. Think and let think." The increasing opposition of the Church of England toward his work, and its expressed hatred for it, compelled Wesley to act independently of it, and so, on July 27, 1730, the first Methodist Society was formed with its own rules of government. Wesley ordained his own preachers. On June 25, 1744, the first Methodist Conference was held in London, with six ministers and four laymen present.

From then on, Wesley's powers were bent on building up a new religious society that might give a lasting and practical form to the ever-increasing enthusiasm of the people. While the whole body was placed under the absolute government of a conference of ministers, as long as he lived, the direction of the new religious society remained in Wesley's hand. Replying with a charming simplicity to those who objected to his autocratic control, he said, "If by arbitrary power you mean a power which I exercise simply without any colleagues there in, this is certainly true, but I see no hurt in it." C. H. Spurgeon is credited with having said that he believed in a committee of one, the one being himself.

HIS MARITAL PROBLEMS

John Wesley had had such a happy, godly home life, with so many other children around him in his childhood days, that he must have longed for a similar home of his own, with children to rise up and call him blessed. Yet his experience with women with a view to matrimony was not a very satisfactory one. Sally Kirkham, daughter of the Rector of Stanton, Gloucestershire, who encouraged Wesley to become a Church of England minister, was referred to as "a religious friend." Whatever feelings they had toward each other we are not told. She faded from the picture, however. Then, there was Grace Murray, to whom Wesley became attached after being nursed by her through an illness. In fact, they became engaged, but friends intervened, and she married another. Grace was the housekeeper at the Newcastle headquarters, and his brother Charles, not knowing the full circumstances of his brother's engagement yet afraid that Methodism would suffer, persuaded Grace Murray to marry one of Wesley's preachers, John Bennet. Pressed by his friends to make the matter a legal issue, Wesley refused. Writing to her, Wesley said, "Grace Murray, you have broken my heart."

When he went on his mission to Georgia, a venture that did not prove to be altogether successful, he formed an attachment to Sophy Hopkey, niece of the chief magistrate of Savannah; but she married someone else. Unwisely, Wesley courted criticism by prohibiting her from partaking of Holy Communion. The misunderstandings and persecutions brought to a head by this Sophy Hopkey affair were one reason Wesley left Savannah for London in December 1737. Wesley then wrote a tract recommending celibacy. Shortly after this, however, he met Mrs. Mary Vageillo, a widow with four children. Brokenhearted over the loss of Grace Murray and on the rebound, he married the widow in 1751, with disastrous results. Wesley stipulated that he was not to preach or to travel less, but his wife became dissatisfied with his continual absences.

Further, Mrs. Wesley became jealous and bitterly resented her husband's intimate pastoral oversight of hundreds of young women, something she scolded him about continually. Wesley, having a high opinion of marital authority, wrote to her and said, "Suspect me no more, asperse me no more, provoke me no more. Do not any longer contend for the mastery: be content to be a private, insignificant person, known and loved by God and me."

Mary left her husband several times, but he always induced her to return to him—until the time when she left him again and he besought her no more. He wrote, "I did not dismiss her, I will not recall her." She died in 1771, and Wesley lived on for another twenty years, untroubled by marital problems. What hurt him most during this affair was perhaps the attitude of his brother Charles during the scandal caused by Mrs. Wesley's publication of stolen, interpolated, or forged letters. Charles was in a fever of excitement over the matter and felt John should do something to defend his character. But John, master of the situation, said to Charles, "Brother, when I devoted to God my ease, my time, my life, did I exempt my reputation?"

One wonders what would have happened if John Wesley had married a godly woman in full sympathy with his glorious task and cheered his heart with children of his own. Seeing that the supreme task of evangelism overshadowed all else in Wesley's life, enabling him to stem the rising tide of a bloody revolution in the land, perhaps his unfortunate marriage was a blessing in disguise.

HIS SPIRITUAL QUEST

Although reared in the godliest of homes and closely identified with religious activities at Oxford and after, Wesley did not have the assurance of a personal Savior. He felt that he could not promote holiness in others until he had achieved it himself, and he believed he could best do this at Oxford. But it was not to be so. The text that kept coming to his mind was Mark 12:34: "*Thou art not far from the kingdom of God.*" In his inmost heart, however, he knew he was not in that kingdom. Then, something happened that was to prompt a chain of events ending in his definite conversion. After the death of his father, he took his monumental Latin work on Job to London to consult with publishers about having it translated and printed. While in the city, he met an old Oxford friend, John Burton, who had become the most influential trustee of the new British colony of Georgia, in North America. Burton introduced him to Col. James Oglethorpe, governor of the colony, and both men persuaded

Wesley to return with them and undertake the spiritual oversight of the colonists, as well as to evangelize the Indians as an agent for the "Society of the Propagation of the Gospel." Wesley accepted, and his brother Charles was ordained in order to accompany him and serve alongside. John told the two friends, "My chief motive is the hope of saving my own soul. I hope to learn the true sense of the gospel by preaching it to the heathen. I cannot hope to attain to the same degree of holiness here which I may there."

Crossing the Atlantic, John and Charles became acquainted with some emigrant Moravians who clearly possessed the spiritual peace John had hitherto sought in vain. On board was the notable Moravian preacher Spangenburg, who dealt with Wesley about his soul. The faith and calmness of the Moravians during several stormy days at sea greatly impressed the Wesleys. The party landed in America on February 6, 1736.

Alas! After two years of hard labor, the mission to the Indians proved somewhat abortive. Both John and Charles had served them and the colonists faithfully, but the stiff, high churchmanship they sought to impose antagonized the people, and their efforts at social changes and spiritual fellowship were rejected. Heartsick, the Wesleys returned to England in 1738, with John seeking ever more doggedly after the truth. Despairing, he wrote, "No such faith in Christ as will prevent my heart being troubled—I went to America to convert the Indians, but oh! Who shall convert me? I have a fair summer religion: I can talk well, but let death look me in the face and my spirit is troubled." In spite of all the trials and failures of Georgia, Wesley looked upon the two years there as "the second rise of Methodism"—the first being the Holy Club at Oxford. The weekly fellowship meetings he had organized in Savannah were, as he said, "the first rudiments of the Methodist societies."

On the sea voyage home, Wesley was again brought into contact with the Moravians, people of tranquil faith. During a storm that threatened disaster, these saints were calm. "Why be disturbed by the waves and the winds?" they said. "God will take care of us all." This was the inner peace the forlorn missionary craved but could not find. He arrived in England on February 1, 1738, only to find that his friend George Whitefield had sailed for America the day before to assist him in his work among the Indians in Georgia. Characteristically, on the way up from Deal to London, Wesley preached and read prayers at several places. Inwardly, however, he was still troubled by a sense of sin and a lack of assurance of forgiveness. The great change that overtook his religious feelings is best told in his own words:

> It is upward of two years since I left my native country, in order to teach the Georgian Indians the nature of Christianity, but what have I learned, myself, in the meantime? Why, what I least of all suspected, that I, who went to America to convert others, was never converted myself.... All this time that I was at Savannah I was beating the air. Being ignorant of the righteousness of Christ, which by a living faith in him, bringing salvation to everyone that believeth, I sought to establish my own righteousness, and so labored in the fire all my days.

But on May 24, 1738, the miracle happened. In the morning, he opened his Bible haphazardly to Mark 12:34 and read again the verse he had often pondered: *"Thou art not far from the kingdom of God."* He was deeply moved by the Master's word to the rich young ruler. In the afternoon, he attended a service in Saint Paul's Cathedral and was further impressed by the singing of the anthem form of Psalm 130: *"Out of the depths have I cried unto thee, O Lord"* (verse 1). But at night, the despairing Church of England clergyman made his way to a small gathering of Moravians and other believers in Aldersgate Street, London. Someone was reading the Preface to Martin Luther's exposition of *The Epistle to the Romans*, and the phrase that gripped Wesley was, "By faith the heart is cheered, elevated, excited, and transported with sweet affections towards God."

Immediately, it seemed as if his chains fell off, and he spoke thereafter of this experience as his conversion. "I felt my heart strangely warmed. I felt I did trust in Christ, Christ alone, for salvation, and an assurance was given me that He had taken my sins, even mine, and saved me from the law of sin and death: and then I testified openly to all there what I now first felt in my heart." About ten that night, he cried, "I believe!" Lecky the historian says that "the conversion of John Wesley formed one of the grand epochs of English history." Wesley had studied closely William Law's book *Serious Call*, and after his conversion, he wrote Law a strong letter, reproving him for not showing him the way of salvation before.

Wesley had to stand a good deal of scorn for his professed change of life. One critic wrote, "If you have not been a Christian ever since I knew you, you have been a hypocrite; for you made us all believe that you were one."

Some three weeks after this conversion experience, Wesley retired to Germany to spend some time with the godly Moravians in their settlement. On his return to England in 1739, he began his open-air preaching, and mighty things happened. He had been urged often by George Whitefield to share his "ministry of the open air," but Wesley had shrunken from preaching outdoors with "a pile of stones as pulpit." Now, however, Wesley took the plunge and became renowned as the Evangelist of the Highways and Byways of England. Although he was only five feet four in height, he commanded the attention of the crowds assembled to hear him. Something about his manner and voice gripped the audience, as his words flowed as clear as a bell to the outer rim of the throng. Wesley was about thirty-five years of age and had been a clergyman for ten years at the time he came to see that the rest of his life must be spent as a herald of salvation by faith.

HIS MANIFOLD GIFTS

From the dawn of his new life, Wesley dedicated all that he was and all that he had to the furtherance of the gospel. A quaint saying of one of the earliest Methodists was, "I do love those one-eyed Christians," referring to the biblical phrase of "a single eye to the glory of God." This became Wesley's trait. He wore his hair long to save the money for the Lord's work and lived a life of austerity and activity. First of all, he dedicated his time to Him who was the length of his days. "Leisure and I have taken leave of one another. I propose to be busy as long as I live, if my health is so long indulged in me." On one occasion, he spoke plainly to his preachers, telling them that they should do one of three things: "Either spend time in chitchat or learn Latin or Hebrew, or spend all your time and strength in saving souls. Which will you do?" The hearers replied, "The last, by the grace of God." Wesley practiced what he preached, for he knew how to make the most of a day. Once, when he had to wait for a carriage, he said, "I have lost ten minutes forever." Although he appeared to be always in haste, he declared himself never to be in a hurry. The amazing amount of work he completed could have been accomplished only by the most rigid use of each minute. The strain would have broken most men, but Wesley's resolution to redeem the time urged him forward, and his health remained good until about three years before his death.

Wesley practiced a strict economy of time, believing with the apostle Paul that he must redeem the time, seeing the days were evil. (See Ephesians 5:16.) In a letter to Boswell, Samuel Johnson wrote, "John Wesley's conversation is good, but he is never at leisure. He is always obliged to go at a certain hour. This is very disagreeable to a man who loves to fold his legs and have out his talk, as I do."

This tireless preacher would rise at four in the morning for prayer and meditation, preach his first sermon by five, and be on the road by six, riding horseback often sixty to seventy miles and preaching at least three times a day. And he demanded the same strict regimen of his preachers. Any man who felt he could not gladly rise at four in the morning and be ready to preach to needy souls at five was no worker of his. He stoutly condemned laziness.

In Wesley's day, the English clergy were the idlest and most lifeless in the world. By one observer, they were branded as "the most remiss of their labors in private, and the least severe in their lives." No wonder these lazy clerics were awakened to strong opposition to Wesley's strict discipline and indefatigable industry! His full use of time for God shamed them. He knew how to give each flying minute something to keep in store.

Wesley also believed in dedicating money to the Lord. He condemned wasting money on drink, tobacco, and extravagant dress. One year, he spent five pounds nineteen shillings on himself and six hundred pounds in charity for the needy. Throughout his wonderful career, his asceticism was like that of a monk. At times, he lived on bread only, and he often slept on bare boards. Yet, it must be remembered that in spite of the rough-and-tumble world in which Wesley lived, he never restricted his devotion to learning. He mastered six languages and studied their best literature. In the saddle on his long rides, he read the classics or made shorthand notes for his voluminous daily journal that became a spiritual classic. One of Wesley's biographers says,

> The inconveniences and dangers which he embraced that he might preach the Gospel and do good of every kind to all that would receive it at his hands; the exposing of himself to every change of season and inclemency of weather in the prosecution of his work, were conditions which few but himself could have submitted to. He frequently slept on the ground as he journeyed through woods, covered with the nightly dews, and with his clothes and his hair frozen, in the morning, to the earth. He would wade through swamps and swim through rivers, and then travel

till his clothes were dry. His health, strange as it may seem, was uninterrupted.

As a preacher, evangelist, and teacher, Wesley was eminently used of God. His presentation of truth was both doctrinal and practical. Pattison says of Wesley's preaching that "violent ranting was as offensive to him as was heartless reasoning." In preparing for the pulpit, he wrote much, but he did not read his sermons. He expanded or contracted his material as the occasion demanded. The arrangement of his thoughts was admirable. To systematize was as natural with him as to breathe. He spoke, as he lived, by rule.

> On board ship, at the mouth of a coal pit, amid the distractions of a country fair, surrounded by thousands of rough miners in the natural amphitheatre of the Cornish hillside, Wesley never seems to have failed to make himself understood. His slight, compact figure, his flowing silver locks, his benignant countenance, his clear, resonant utterances, immediately impressed his hearers with a sense of authority, and needed not the clerical garb which he always wore to command respect. His voice and his gesture were not dramatic, his manner was that of a man of fearless spirit, of intense earnestness, and of rare spiritual fervor. Robert Hall said of him, "While he set all things in motion, he was himself perfectly calm; he was the quiescence of turbulence."

Wesley had a unique gift as an organizer and became identified with many causes. His genius for organization was recognized by Macaulay, who described him as one "whose genius for government was not inferior to that of Richelieu." Yet, as the eminent Methodist preacher Dr. Dinsdale T. Young points out in his admirable volume on *Popular Preaching*, it was

> John Wesley's popular preaching, rather than his organizing genius, which, speaking after the manner of men,

founded Methodism....That John Wesley was a great popular preacher can never be successfully disputed....Where he found the secret of popular preaching all preachers will discover....It is at the Cross of Christ that this transcendent worth is discovered....If preachers live at Calvary, I do not shrink from saying, they possess the secret of popular preaching. Nowhere else is that inestimable secret to be learned.

As a writer, Wesley had a gifted pen that wielded a tremendous influence for God and righteousness. He was as versatile as he was intense. He published grammars in at least five languages, issued a library of religious literature, and even wrote a novel. His famous *Journal* is still the best history of the rise of Methodism, and his written sermons the best compendium of its theology. Wesley's incomparable *Journal* was described by Augustine Birrell as "the most amazing record of human experience ever penned or endured...a book full of plots and plays and novels, which quiver with life and is full of character." In 1778, he founded a monthly magazine, a weapon in his theological warfare with the Calvinists. Then, there is also his *Primitive Physic*, a book that reads quaintly today but, because of its plain practicability, went through nearly a hundred editions in as many years.

There is a most interesting sequel: Wesley sent a copy of this family medicine book for the poor folks to Dr. Hawes, a well-known London physician. He bitterly attacked it as being full of magic and ignorance. His adverse review boosted the sales of the book so much that Wesley wrote to him,

Dear Sir, My bookseller informs me that since you have published your remarks on the *Primitive Physic, or an Essay and Natural Method of Curing Most Diseases*, there has been a greater demand for it than ever. If, therefore, you would please publish a few further remarks, you would confer a further favour upon your humble servant, J. Wesley.

This medical work, stressing plain food, fresh air, abundant exercise, and a contented spirit, netted Wesley thousands of pounds, which he ploughed back into publishing the book for free distribution. His four hundred publications, covering all sorts of topics, followed the broad conception of doing good to all men, to their bodies and minds as well as to their souls. This Christian library summarized in fifty volumes "the choicest pieces of practical divinity in the English tongue, especially skimming the cream from the somewhat longwinded writings of the Puritans.

"No man in the eighteenth century did so much to create a good taste for good reading, and to supply it with books at the lowest prices than Wesley." He had a skill and learning in writing none of the other Methodists possessed, which is further seen in the quality of *Rules*, published in 1743, to avoid the scandal of having unworthy members in his society. Possessing and reading this book was a condition of acceptance as a member. It listed evil practices to be avoided and inculcated positive forms of social service and regular use of the various means of grace. Members who habitually broke these rules were expelled from membership. Though slavery was protected by law and considered highly respectable in his day, Wesley did not hesitate to fight it. His volume *Thoughts upon Slavery* did for England what Harriet Beecher Stowe's *Uncle Tom's Cabin* did for America.

Then, there was his work *Compendium of Natural Philosophy*, in which he wrote on the habits of beasts, birds, and insects. Years before Charles Darwin, Wesley leaned toward evolution, concluding that "there is a prodigious number of continued links between the most perfect man and the ape."

Wesley gave away forty thousand pounds—a terrific sum in those days—in royalties from his books and pamphlets, and he limited himself to thirty pounds a year for personal expenses. He once said that he would give people the privilege of calling him a robber if at the time of his death he owned more than ten pounds.

As a hymn writer, he was next to his brother Charles in output. Many of the hymns John composed will live as long as our language. He believed that Methodism was raised up "to spread Scriptural holiness over the land," and his hymns, along with the three thousand or more Charles Wesley wrote, greatly helped in such an effort. In the revivals under the Wesleys, we are apt to stress a division of labor between the two brothers and to speak of John as the preacher and Charles as the hymn writer. "But this is not strictly accurate," says Julian in his mammoth *Dictionary of Hymnology*:

> On the one hand Charles was also a great preacher, second only to his brother and George Whitefield in the effects which he produced. On the other hand, John by no means relegated to Charles the exclusive task of supplying the people with their hymns….When he speaks of the hymns, it is, "My brother and I." He saw at once that hymns might be utilized, not only for raising the devotion, but also for instructing and establishing the faith of his disciples…. The part which John played in actually writing the hymns is not easy to ascertain, but it is certain that more than thirty translations from the German, French, and Spanish were exclusively his; and there are some original hymns, admittedly his composition, which are not unworthy to stand by the side of his brother's.

The hymns of the Wesleys expressed the fiery conviction of their converts in lines so chaste and beautiful that its more extravagant features disappeared. "The wild throes of hysteric enthusiasm passed into a passion for hymn-singing, and a new musical impulse was aroused in the people which gradually changed the face of public devotion through England."

As an organizer and administrator, John Wesley was without peer. He controlled the various societies he had created as a statesman would. He labored on, unwearied, and the flame of revival spread. Converts became so numerous that Wesley's powers were bent to the building up of a great religious society that might give to the new enthusiasm a lasting and practical form. Thus, his followers were "grouped into classes, gathered in love-feasts, and purified by the expulsion of unworthy members, and furnished with an alternation of settled ministers and wandering preachers." J. R. Green goes on to say that "the great body which he thus founded—a body which numbered a hundred thousand members at his death, and which now counts its members by millions— bears the stamp of Wesley in more than its name."

Wesley's spiritual and beneficial creations were most remarkable. Not only was he the founder and director of a great religious movement, but he was also the founder of England's first free medical dispensary—the forerunner of the national health system. To give employment to the poor, he organized various outlets such as spinning and knitting shops. He actually established Wesley's Benevolent Loan Fund to help finance new business enterprises, as well as The Strangers' Friend Society, which offered relief to "poor, sick, friendless strangers." As the result of his monumental activities, a wonderful philanthropic movement began after his death— Sunday schools by Raikes, Hannah More's fight against poverty and crime, Wilberforce's crusade against slavery, and Howard's far-reaching reform of prisons, which was an extension of Wesley's fight against a horrible system of filth, starvation, and degradation.

HIS CONSTANT PERSECUTION

Although a great and effective door had opened to John Wesley, he came to experience that with it were many adversaries. This realization compelled him to write, "A Christian will be despised anywhere, and no one is a Christian till he is despised."

At one place where he preached, he was mobbed, and the cry arose, "Knock out his brains! Kill him at once!" The leader of the gang intervened and rescued Wesley. "Tuberculosis threatened him, mobs stoned him, churchmen denounced him, and his own sensitive nature cringed from the roughness of the life he led. But with faith aflame he rode on to accomplish his purposes." His ruthless denunciation of drunkenness and immorality aroused fierce hostility. As crowds gathered to hear the Wesleys preach, antagonists would let loose vicious animals to stampede the people gathered for worship and ministry. Drunken mobs would attack the meeting houses of the Methodists with stones and clubs. Charles Wesley said that he could identify the homes of Methodists by the marks of missiles hurled against them.

There was an occasion when John Wesley was stoned by a mob, but, although beaten to the ground, he prayed with such fervor that his attackers were silenced. Prizefighter George Clifton, leader of the mob, put his hand on Wesley's head and said, "Sir, I will spend my life for you. Not one soul shall harm a hair of your head." Completely reformed by grace, this man became not only Wesley's bodyguard but also an ardent Methodist preacher. "Mobs might pursue him with stones, but Wesley would retreat with a deliberateness which was in itself victorious, and, once there, would comb out his white locks, and find relief in the pages of his *Horace*."

Although Wesley was a clergyman of the Episcopal Church and never failed to respect her in spite of the rejection she caused him to suffer, yet because of the nature of his deep revival preaching, the church closed her pulpits to him, and he was forced to preach in barns and fields. Preaching that could move the hearts of grimy miners at the pithead and cause them to weep, "making white channels down their blackened cheeks," was more than an apathetic church could stand. Still, if Wesley could not preach in a church, he would take to the churchyard; if excluded from that, there was the village green. The Established Church gave him no encouragement or consideration. The church in which his father, his brother Charles, and he himself had been ordained was closed against him. At Epworth Church, where his father had ministered, the curate would not allow him to enter the building, saying, "Tell Mr. Wesley I shall not give him the sacrament, for he is not fit." With this refusal, Wesley put up a notice in the grave-yard saying that he would preach there at six. A crowd assembled to hear him preach from where he stood, on his father's grave. Afterward, he wrote, "I am well assured that I did far more good to my Lincolnshire parishioners by preaching three days on my father's tomb than I did by preaching three years in his pulpit." Closed churches could not check the rising tide of revival. Such opposition only forced it into new channels, and Wesley feared none save for God, his determination being:

> By all Hell's host withstood:
> We all Hell's host o'erthrow:
> And conquering them through Jesus' blood,
> We on to victory go.[10]

HIS TRIUMPHANT DEATH

In spite of his rigid, disciplined life, exposure to all kinds of weather, and unceasing trials and persecutions, he reached his eighty-eighth milestone on the pilgrimage of life. To the very last, he preached and wrote daily. On his deathbed, he called out, "Where is my sermon on the love of God? Take it and spread it abroad. Give it to everyone."

His life from 1703 to 1791 almost spanned the century; he had lived to see the Methodist body pass through every phase of its history before he sank into his grave. As he reached his eighti-eth year, he remarked that he could not remember having felt low-ness of spirits for one quarter of an hour since he was born. "By the grace of God, I never fret; I repine at nothing; I am discontented at

10. Charles Wesley, "Angels Your March Oppose," 1749.

nothing." And he died, even as he had lived, calm and content. In the week of his death, he rose at four each day, preached, and traveled, as usual, until the Wednesday, when he preached for the last time, at Leatherhead, Surrey. On Friday, symptoms appeared that left little doubt as to the imminence of his end, and he spent the next four days praising God. His leading preachers were gathered around his bed, and his last words to them and to the world were these: "The best of all is, God is with us." At ten on Tuesday morning, March 2, 1791, he heard the divine voice say, "Come up hither," and God took His valiant servant home. After lying in state in his ministerial robes at his chapel in City Road, London, he was buried there on March 9.

The burial of John Wesley was in keeping with his conviction about service to others. He had said that men could call him a robber if he left more than ten pounds at his death. He had drawn up instructions for his burial, and these were carried out to the letter. He was buried in nothing more costly than wool, and whatever money remained in his box or pockets was to be given to his followers. As a protest against needless funeral expenses, he had ordered that no hearse be employed and that six poor men in need of work be hired at one pound each to carry his body to the grave. It was reckoned that over ten thousand of his followers gathered to say farewell to their honored leader.

Although the church had closed her doors against him, at his end, Wesley was an honored figure throughout the British Isles. Today on the wall of Westminster Abbey, you will see the medallion of his face and that of his brother Charles—one, the most successful popular gospel preacher; one, the sweetest poet of their generation. Below the medallion are three sentences expressing the spirit of John Wesley and embodying his faith:

I look on all the World as my parish.
God buries His workmen, but continues His work.

Then come the last words that broke from his lips in death:

The best of all is, God is with us.

At Wesley's death, there were Methodist Societies all over Britain, three hundred traveling preachers, seventy-two thousand members of Societies, and about five hundred thousand adherents. About two thirds lived overseas, especially in America, where membership continued to grow at a far more rapid rate than in Wesley's homeland. For many years, those following Wesley's teachings were known as Wesleyans. They were members of the Nonconformist Church he had founded around 1739. The main lesson of Wesley's life was "Be Earnest! Be Earnest." And what an intense devotion was his! "No single figure influenced so many minds: no single voice touched so many hearts." With all his consecrated heart John Wesley believed that

> 'Tis not in man to trifle, life is brief,
> And sin is here.
> Our age is but the falling of a leaf,
> A passing tear.[11]

Scores of able writers, Methodists and others, have described the marvelous expansion of Methodism since Wesley's day. It remains for us to say only that all the voluminous literature on Wesley and his work is the preeminent testimony to his exemplary life and prodigious labors. He still lives on in the religious community that, under the Spirit's power, he brought into being. A wise man of the world remarked, "When Mr. Wesley drops, all this is at an end." But Wesley himself replied, "So it will, unless before God calls him home one is found to stand in his place."

When he was called home, there were many able, godly men ready to take his place and carry the torch forward. Certainly, they were not of the same caliber as John Wesley, for when God

---

11. Hortius Bonar, "'Tis Not for Man to Trifle."

made him, He broke the mold. But the three hundred preachers he left behind were singularly blessed by God in spreading the flame. Today, over 180 years after Wesley's death, there are some eighteen million members of the Methodist Church scattered over the world, with an unofficial membership or constituency of more than forty million persons. In Great Britain, there are about a million members, but in America, the Methodist Church boasts nearly ten million members, as well as three large African-American Methodist bodies with about two-and-a-half-million members. Altogether, there are twenty-six separate Methodist bodies in the United States, of which the Methodist Church is numerically the strongest, with its numerous churches, universities, colleges, schools, hospitals, and homes for the aged. It holds property worth more than 3 billion dollars. But the influence of this prominent Protestant denomination cannot be read in its statistics. In the main, the evangelistic passion for conversion, righteous living, and social welfare, so characteristic of Wesley's long ministry, still operates in the religious society he founded, causing it to be a mighty spiritual factor in a world of sin and need.

One cannot meditate upon the life and service of John Wesley without being deeply impressed with what God is able to accomplish through a man as utterly yielded to Him as this consecrated clergyman was. Believing that a loving God had every claim upon his time and talents, he dedicated them entirely to Him for the accomplishment of His redemptive plan for a lost world. By the grace of God, may we be found following the stirring example of John Wesley!

CHAPTER 8

CHARLES HADDON SPURGEON: THE PRINCE OF GOSPEL PREACHERS

King Solomon warned us that the name of the wicked will rot. (See Proverbs 10:7.) He also reminded us that the name of the righteous is as ointment poured forth. (See Song of Solomon 1:3.) A name retaining its fragrance throughout the last century is that of Charles Haddon Spurgeon, who was one of the most popular and prolific preachers in an age of great preaching, and who will always remain one of the most outstanding figures among evangelical heralds. In the days of his flesh, his ministry was nothing short of a marvel, and his influence abides in the perennial publications of his gospel-drenched sermons. His picture in the portrait gallery of God's world-changing ministers is one of first order. The person who approaches it sympathetically is always repaid.

HIS GODLY HERITAGE

Like so many renowned preachers, Spurgeon came from Christian stock. His grandfather was a Congregational minister greatly used in the salvation of souls. His father also was a minister of this denomination. C. H. Spurgeon was one of eight children. He was born on June 17, 1834, in Kelvedon, Essex. His mother was an uncommonly earnest Christian who took great pains in the shaping of the character of her children. An aunt whom Spurgeon called "Mother Ann" loved him tenderly and fostered him as her own child. After his conversion, he left the Independents and joined the Baptists. His mother was sad over his change, and she told him that she had prayed earnestly for his salvation, but not that he should be a Baptist. Spurgeon replied, "Well, dear Mother, you know that the Lord is so good that He always gives us more than we can ask or think."

The name *Spurgeon* suggests his origin. He sprang from Flemish Huguenots, driven from their native country by persecution and finding refuge in the flatlands in the eastern part of England. It would seem that his ancestry shaped his theology, for while he must have been familiar with John Wesley's writings and work, he went back further, to the Puritans of Europe; in his doctrine and preaching, he was essentially Puritan. Without a doubt, he was steeped in Puritan literature and thus delighted to proclaim grace—free, sovereign, unmerited grace. Toward the end of his ministry, Spurgeon said, "I have been thirty years in one place, but I do not believe I should have been thirty months in one place if it had not been for the gospel."

Although he had the privilege of being raised in a Christian home and had delighted at the age of six delighted to read Bunyan's *Pilgrim's Progress* and his other works, Spurgeon was not yet saved. "I had heard of the plan of salvation by the sacrifice of Jesus from my youth up, but I did not know any more about it in my innermost soul than if I had been born and bred a Hottentot. The light was there, but I was blind. The eyeballs of the soul were not sensitive to the divine beams."

As a child, he manifested evident self-possession, strong passion, and will. His education was somewhat limited, being confined chiefly to a private academy at Colchester that was run by a local Baptist. Later there came a year at an agricultural school in Maidstone. His parents were most eager for him to go to Cambridge, but he refused because he felt called to an active life. Educationally, Spurgeon is a fitting example of God taking the *"things which are not, to bring to nought the things which are"* (1 Corinthians 1:28).

HIS RADICAL CONVERSION

For one so young, Spurgeon had great distress of soul over his spiritual condition. This conviction of sin lasted for about five years. He seemed to have a remarkable consciousness of sin and of the justice of God. Later on in life, referring to this flowing of heart and conscience, he said, "When I was in the hands of the Holy Spirit under conviction of sin, I had a clear and sharp sense of the justice of God." What a lack of this conviction there is today! God spoke in two ways to the young, troubled heart of Spurgeon. "Once God preached to me by the similitude in the depth of winter," he said. Looking upon the black earth, he thought of sin, and in the white snow falling upon it, he saw the Savior and was reminded that although his sins were scarlet, he could be made as white as snow. (See Isaiah 1:18.)

Then, there was the vision he had of a murdered friend, and the search for the murderer, with the pursuers hot on his trail. Relating this experience, Spurgeon said, "At last I put my hand upon my breast: 'I have thee now,' said I: for lo! He was in my own heart; the murderer was hiding within my own bosom." Overwhelmed with guilt, he wept.

> 'Twas you my sins, my cruel sins
> His chief tormentors were:
> Each of my crimes became a nail
> And unbelief a spear.

In order to find peace, Spurgeon read good books explaining a God-provided deliverance from sin—Baxter's *Call to the Unconverted*, James's *Anxious Enquirer*, Doddridge's *Rise and Progress of Religion in the Soul*—but he failed to find relief from his burden of sin. He wandered from church to church but found no message to chase the dark night of sin away. Then, one Sunday morning, unable to reach the church he had meant to visit because of a severe snowstorm, he turned in to a very small country Primitive Methodist Chapel. About fifteen people were present that cold, bleak morning, and the minister who was to preach was held up by the storm. After the consultation of the two or three leaders, "a thin-looking man, a shoemaker or tailor, went up into the pulpit." To Spurgeon, he seemed to be both stupid and uninstructed. When he came to his sermon, he gave out a text but could not read it properly. It was Isaiah 45:22: "*Look unto me, and be ye saved.*" But he did not stick to his text; he could only fasten on the word "*Look.*" He said, "Now, looking don't take a deal of pains. It ain't lifting your foot or your finger, it is just—look! *Me*—look not to yourselves, not to the Spirit working, not to your neighbours, but to Me!" Then the crude, unlettered preacher went on to urge the few worshippers before him to look to the drops of blood from the cross and to Christ risen and ascended. After about ten minutes, he seemed to be at the end of his tether. Then, fixing his eyes upon young Spurgeon sitting under the gallery, the poor substitute for the minister said, "Young man, you look miserable. You will always be miserable in life and miserable in death. Young man, look to Jesus Christ. Look! Look! Look!"

In giving his testimony of what happened on that Sunday morning, January 6, between 10:30 to 12:30, in the year 1850, Spurgeon says, "At once I saw the way of salvation. Oh, I looked until I could almost have looked my eyes away. I looked at Him, He looked at me, and we were one forever." The psalmist says, "*They looked to Him and were radiant*" (Psalm 34:5 NKJV). This was the immediate and radical experience of Spurgeon: "I thought I could dance all the way home. I could understand what John Bunyan meant when he declared he wanted to tell the crows in the ploughed land all about his conversion....I thought I could have sprung from the seat in which I sat and have called out with the wildest of those Methodist brethren who were present, I am forgiven! I am forgiven! A monument of grace. A sinner saved by Blood."

D. L. Moody said that on the day of his conversion, it seemed as if all the birds of the hedgerow sang more joyful songs. G. Campbell Morgan testified that on the day of his spiritual crisis, the leaves of the trees appeared to be more beautiful. It is always so when a guilty soul looks to Jesus and is saved.

> Heaven above is softer blue,
> Earth around is sweeter green;
> Something lives in every hue
> Christless eyes have never seen:
> Birds with gladder songs o'erflow,
> Flow'rs with deeper beauties shine,
> Since I know, as now I know, I am His, and He is mine.

From the very outset of his conversion, Spurgeon had a clear understanding of what it meant to be saved, as these paragraphs prove:

> There is a power in God's gospel beyond all description. In my conversion the very point lay in making the discovery that I had nothing to do but to look to Christ and I should be saved.

> When I was anxious about the possibility of a just God pardoning me, I understood and saw by faith that He who is the Son of God became man and in His own blessed Person bore my sin in His body on the tree.

> The Holy Spirit so enabled me to believe, and gave me peace through believing, that I felt as sure that I was forgiven as before I felt sure of my condemnation.

The blessed assurance was his that he knew whom he had believed, and, by the power of God, Spurgeon became the means of leading countless numbers into the same assurance of faith.

HIS PASTORAL SPHERES

After his unmistakable conversion at the age of fifteen, Spurgeon became deeply interested in baptism. He consulted his Congregationalist father, who, like his mother, was possibly not favorable to the idea. But, convinced that he should be immersed as a witness to his faith in Christ, he walked seven miles from Newmarket to Isleham on May 3, 1850, and was baptized by Pastor Cantlow. At the time, he was tutoring at Mr. Leeding's school. At Newmarket, he had been a scholar, but now he had been removed to Cambridge. Here, young Spurgeon became a member of the Baptist Church in Saint Andrews' Street, where Robert Hall, the renowned Baptist preacher, had so long been pastor.

Spurgeon became a member of the church's "Lay Preacher's Association," which supplied the thirteen small, neighboring churches with preachers. So commenced his preaching career. He preached his first sermon in a cottage at Teversham, and his fame spread quickly. Crowds started gathering to hear "The Boy Preacher," as he became known. The Baptist Church at Waterbeech, a village of about thirteen hundred at that time, called him to be pastor, and at eighteen years of age, he began his pulpit ministry. After his first sermon in this village, an aged voice quavered out, "Bless your dear heart. How old are you?" The sense of quiet humor saved young Spurgeon, for his solemn reply was, "You must wait till the service is over before making any such inquiries. Let us now sing."

The fame of this youthful preacher and his buoyant exhilaration quickly spread. When it reached London, it led to an invitation to preach at the New Park Street Chapel in 1853. When but nineteen years of age, Spurgeon succeeded many Baptist worthies with their long pastorates in this notable church, which, by this time, had become almost empty. His ministry was an instant and remarkable success, and he sprang to the highest rank in the preaching world. Within a year, the church, proud of its past, was far too small for the crowds eager to hear the exceedingly eloquent young preacher. From then on, he was destined for almost forty years to hold a prominent position among English preachers.

Because of the utter inadequacy of the New Park Street Chapel to hold the crowds that flocked to hear Spurgeon, a decision was made to build a large center in the metropolis of Newington Butts. While the Metropolitan Tabernacle was being built, several meeting places were used. Spurgeon often preached to audiences of over ten thousand in the Surrey Gardens Music Hall. His voice was so powerful that he could reach as many as twenty thousand people without effort, and that without our modern-day microphones and public address systems. Said one of his voice, "Its first note, while it filled with ease the largest place, was so personal that each one of his hearers seemed to be personally addressed."

In 1861, the Tabernacle was opened, with seating for some five thousand. At twenty-seven years of age, Spurgeon began a ministry that was phenomenal in every way. Ten years prior, while he had been pastoring a small church at Waterbeach, he rode home one night and watched a lamplighter lighting the streetlamps, although he could not see the lamplighter himself. The thought came to him: "How earnestly do I wish that my life may be spent in lighting one soul after another with the sacred flame of eternal life! I would myself be as much as possible unseen while at my work, and would vanish into the eternal brilliance above when my work is done." For over thirty years in the Metropolitan Tabernacle, London, Spurgeon was a mighty lamplighter for the Master he dearly loved and faithfully served. Eternity alone will reveal how many darkened hearts were illuminated through his ministry. Until his death in 1892, he continually attracted vast congregations, and to the last, no church or hall in the land was large enough to accommodate the crowds of people who desired to hear his clarion voice ring forth with the gospel he lived to proclaim. During World War II, the Tabernacle was destroyed by German bombs. It was finally rebuilt on a much smaller scale.

HIS PULPIT MINISTRY

Dr. Thomas Armitage wrote a sketch of Charles Haddon Spurgeon in *The History of Baptists* while the renowned minister was still alive and active:

> As a preacher, he deals only in what Christ and His Apostles thought worthy of their attention; tells what he knows about God and man, sin and holiness, time and eternity, in pure ringing Saxon; uses voice enough to make people hear, speaks out like a man to men, lodging his words in their ears and hearts, instead of making his own throat or nose their living sepulchre. He fills his mind with old Gospel truth, and his mind with old Puritan thought, calls the fertility of his imagination into use, believes in Jesus Christ with all the power of his being, loves the souls of men with all his heart and acts accordingly. He carries the least amount of religion possible in the white of his eyes, but a living well of it in the depth of his soul, and the real wonder is not that God has put much honour upon him, for if his life had been very different from what it has been, even partial failure in the hands of such a man of God would have been a new and unsolvable mystery in the reign of a faithful Christ.

Spurgeon's constant theme, preached in plain and simple English, was that of a personal salvation through faith in Christ. In the pulpit, he combined sincerity with natural gestures, easy delivery, skillfully told illustration, and, often, humor, which was always homely. An unashamed fundamentalist, he was outspoken against the growth of modes of thought that were antagonistic to the purity of the faith he loved. Because of this, in 1887, owing to his distrust of the modern criticism of Scripture, he felt compelled to sever his connection with the Baptist Union.

Spurgeon was often denounced and bitterly criticized by jealous-minded ministers, but his popularity with the masses never waned, for the simple reason that he preached as one who was confident that the God he knew personally was with him in the pulpit. No one could doubt his unquestioning faith. Puritan certitude was his strength. Everyone who heard him was inspired by his strong and confident faith to witness, steadfast to the end. Always and everywhere he was an evangelistic preacher, and "the common people heard him gladly." With a nature rich in sympathy, he was essentially a preacher to the people. "I am," he said, "neither eloquent nor learned, but the Head of the Church has given me sympathy with the masses, love to the poor, and the means of winning the attention of the ignorant and unenlightened. God has owned me to the most degraded and off-cast; let others serve their class; these are mine, and to them I must keep."

Spurgeon was short in stature and unimpressive in appearance—his redeeming facial feature was an eye at once brilliant and kindly. Spurgeon had a remarkable voice, clarion in its power to rouse the hearts of large audiences. "His ear for harmony was so perfect that each sentence was complete as it fell from his lips." After hearing him, a professor at Edinburgh University said, "I feel that it would do me good to hear the like of that, it sat so close to reality." Oratorical powers he undoubtedly had, but the orator was forgotten in the prophet, and it was because he was God's messenger in God's message that he was able to preach before eight to ten thousand persons every Sunday in the greatest city in the world. The *London Spectator* said of him, "It is evident that the great oratorical gifts which he undoubtedly possesses are accompanied by solid powers of thought, by imagination, and by humour."

HIS LITERARY LEGACY

Spurgeonic literature never loses its appeal. This is evidenced by its continual appearance from evangelical publishing houses. How grateful we are that his sermons are still being printed—a phenomenon of literature if ever there was one! In his lifetime, thirty-eight volumes of them were issued, and interest in them has not died out. Millions upon millions of Spurgeon's sermons have been sold. He carefully revised every sermon before publication, a task occupying one full day every week. In every volume of his sermons, there are discourses of rare power, and all in greater or lesser degree show the affluence of his mind. Dr. Robertson Nicoll, who urged preachers to soak themselves in Spurgeon's writings, said of his sermons, "Our children will think more of them than we do; and as I get older I read them more and more. He stood at the heart of things."

Among the numerous stories told of the abiding value and appeal of Spurgeon's printed sermons is the one I came across in W. Robertson Nicoll's biography of Dr. John Watson, who, under the pen name Ian Maclaren, authored some of the finest Scottish stories ever written. Describing the powerful evangelical forces in the life of Watson, Robertson Nicoll tells of the Blairgowrie farm where Watson made acquaintance with Spurgeon's sermons, and of how he related it in one of his happiest sketches, which we herewith cull from Nicoll's charming biography of his friend.

Watson tells how the Blairgowrie farmer was told by his good wife to bring home from the market town the tea and sugar, the paraffin oil, and other necessities of life. "And, John, dinna forget Spurgeon." Spurgeon was the weekly number of the Metropolitan Tabernacle Pulpit. As the provident woman had written every requirement— except the oil, which was obtained at the ironmongers's, and the Spurgeon, which was sold at the draper's—on a sheet of paper, and pinned it on the topmost cabbage leaf that covered the butter, the risk was not great; but that week the discriminating prophecy of the good man's capabilities seemed to be justified, for the oil was there, but

Spurgeon could not be found. It was not in the bottom of the dogcart, nor below the cushion, nor attached to a piece of saddlery, nor even in the good man's trousers pocket—all familiar resting places—and when it was at last extricated from the inner pocket of his top coat, a garment with which he had no intimate acquaintance, he received no credit, for it was pointed out with force that to have purchased the sermon and then to have mislaid it was worse than forgetting it altogether. "The Salvation of Manasseh," read the good wife; "it would have been a fine-like business to have missed that; a'll warrant this'll be ane o' his sappiest, but they're a' gude." And then Manasseh was put in a prominent and honorable place, behind the basket of wax flowers in the best parlor till Sabbath. When Sabbath came, the lads from the bothie were brought into the kitchen and entertained to tea. Then afterward, the master of the house read a sermon by Spurgeon. On that particular evening, the little gathering was held in the loft because it was harvest time and extra men were working. It was laid on the boy as an honor to read Manasseh.

"Whether the sermon is called by this name I do not know, and whether it be one of the greatest of Mr. Spurgeon's, I do not know, nor have I a copy of it; but it was mighty unto salvation in that loft, and I make no doubt that good grain was garnered unto eternity. There is a passage in it when, after the mercy of God has rested on this chief sinner, an angel flies through the length and breadth of heaven, crying, 'Manasseh is saved, Manasseh is saved.' Up to that point the lad read, and further he did not read. You know, because you have been told, how insensible and careless is a schoolboy, how destitute of all sentiment and emotion…and therefore I do not ask you to believe me. You know how dull and stupid is a plowman, because you have been told…and therefore I do not ask you to believe me.

"It was the light which got into the lad's eyes and the dust which choked his voice, and it must have been for the same reasons that a plowman passed the back of his hand across his eyes.

"'Ye'll be tired noo,' said the good man; 'lat me feenish the sermon,' but the sermon is not yet finished, and never shall be."

Watson was brought up under powerful evangelical influences, and there can be no doubt that they touched him to the core of his heart. But it is right to say that his mother was of a broader school. He himself wrote in 1905, "My mother, I believe, would have gladly seen me a minister of the Established Church. She was a moderate in theology, and had a rooted dislike to amateur preachers and all their ways, believing that if you employed a qualified physician rather than a quack for your body, you had better have a qualified clergyman rather than a layman for your soul. From her, I received the main principles of my religious thinking. She taught me that all doctrine must be tried by human experience, and that if it was not proved by our reason and conscience, it was not true; and especially I learned from her to believe in the Fatherhood of God and to argue from the human home to the divine family. She always insisted that as we were all the children of one Father, He would make the best of us, both in this world and that which is to come. This, however, was the theology of the Moderate school, and not of the Free Church." He also draws the contrast between the two churches as they appeared to him in early days. "The Free Church of that day was more intense, dogmatic, self-righteous, and evangelistic; the spirit of the Established Church was more liberal and humane, and possibly some would add less spiritual. I greatly honored the leading Free Church."

Another illustration of the influence of Spurgeon's printed messages can be found in Arthur Porritt's illuminating biography of Dr. J. H. Jowett, who was one of the most accomplished pulpiteers of his time. John Loosemore, one of his most intimate friends, wrote of Jowett's Saturday preparation of his Sunday services at Carr's Lane, Birmingham, and how very early on the Sunday morning, Jowett would read "one of Spurgeon's sermons, for the sake of its atmosphere. Then he would arrive at Carr's Lane, bearing in his mind the ordered and familiar results of a week's honest toil and in his heart the glorious purpose of the Christian redemption."

Spurgeon read widely, could gather material rapidly, and knew where to put it in order to have it at command when needed. His mind was both quick and retentive. A study of his printed works proves this. Think of his monumental expositions of the Psalms— *The Treasury of David*—without doubt one of the greatest works on the Psalter. Then we have his *Salt Cellars, Plain Advice for Plain People, John Ploughman's Talks, Commentary on Commentaries, Art of Illustration, Lectures to Students*, and his famous *Autobiography* in four volumes. Then, there was the magazine he founded, *Sword and Trowel*. All of these, like his sermons, have had astronomical sales.

HIS BENEFICIAL INSTITUTIONS

The labors of Spurgeon were varied. Not content with his herculean responsibilities as the pastor of the largest church in the land, special preacher all over the country, and author of numerous books, he launched out for the Master in other directions, in which his talent for organization and administration became evident. Early in life, he already had a passion for books, and this became more intense. It led him to form a "Colportage Society," made up of earnest soulwinners who, as colporteurs, went from house to house selling and distributing religious tracts and books. In this way, he scattered silent messengers of the gospel far and wide.

Then, with a heart full of tenderness for the poor, neglected children of that time, he founded the "Spurgeon Orphanages" and in this way extended his spiritual influence. Distressed by the plight of many old people, he instituted almshouses for them, where they were tenderly cared for in the evening tide of their life.

Entering the ministry, as he did, without any theological training, out of sympathy for young men not able to pay for their lodging and preparation for church work, he created Spurgeon's College. Perhaps another motive he had for founding such a center for the spiritual and mental equipment of men for the ministry was the way that many other theological schools then were beginning to adopt the liberal, rationalistic approach to Scripture—a movement he strenuously opposed. He wanted to produce men who would revere and preach the Bible as he did, and he was successful in his purpose. Through his own preaching over the land, small churches sprang up, and the pulpits of these were filled with young men who, after sitting at the feet of this prince of gospel preachers, went out to proclaim the same evangel. This famous Baptist college still flourishes and is perhaps the most conservative of Baptist colleges in England. During the last century, many of the outstanding preachers in the Baptist denomination studied there, and their roll call is most impressive.

HIS PREMATURE END

We use the word *premature*, meaning "a happening before the proper or usual time, or, too early," about Spurgeon, who died before he was fifty-eight years of age. The psalmist reminds us that the normal span of life is threescore years and ten. Had this renowned preacher, whose influence is still felt, lived another ten years, one wonders what mightier things he might have accomplished for the cause of Christ. But, in the divine counsels, Spurgeon's death was not before God's time; for He is the length of our days, whether they are few or many. Knowing that his times were in God's hands, Spurgeon was prepared for his transition to glory. He was often ill, and as the shadow deepened, often forcing him to leave England in search of sunshine, he sensed that his time was short. His last words, spoken in his dear Tabernacle on June 7, 1891, were as characteristic of any that he ever uttered:

> If you wear the livery of Christ, you will find Him so meek and lowly of heart that you will find rest to your souls. There never was His like among the choicest of princes. He is always to be found in the thickest of the battle. When the wind blows cold, He always takes the bleak side of the hill. The heaviest end of the cross lies ever on His shoulders....His service is life, peace, and joy. God help you to enlist under the banner of Jesus Christ.

Commenting on these last words of Spurgeon, Professor Harwood Pattison says, "As a model of style, rich in illustration, perfect in euphony, these sentences have rarely been excelled. As a summing up of his whole ministry, the ministry of reconciliation, they are complete."

The facts of his last illness and death have been related by all biographers of Spurgeon. He had a wonderful hold on the heart of Christendom. This was evident in the concern for him when he was forced to relinquish his great task. To quote Pattison again, "The Greek patriarch, princes and prelates of the Roman Church, Archbishop and Bishop of the Anglican Church, the Heir-Apparent to the British Throne, the ministers of his own and all other denominations, statesmen and merchants, with multitudes of less known but not less loving hearts, were constant in the expression of their anxiety for his recovery." But it was not to be, for "the time of the singing of birds had come," and for the happy warrior, the winter of his pain was about to vanish.

A long period was spent at Mentone, on the Mediterranean, to which he often retreated when illness struck, and it was while he was here, almost at the same time when his people at the Tabernacle gathered in a thanksgiving service for their beloved pastor's partial recovery, that word reached them that on January 31, 1892, their "Mr. Valiant-for-the-truth" had "passed over, and all the trumpets sounded for him on the other side." Sorrow over his death was universal. Multitudes of consolatory messages reached Mrs. Spurgeon, the Prince and Princess of Wales being among the first to "desire to express their deep sympathy with her in her great sorrow."

It is reckoned that over 100,000 people attended the various memorial and funeral services held at the Tabernacle, where his magnetic voice would be heard no more. When the coffin, with the Bible Charles Haddon Spurgeon had long used opened at Isaiah 45:22—the verse God had used in his salvation over forty years before—passed through the streets, there were very many who recalled the prophetic picture he had given at the close of a sermon he had preached eighteen years before, on December 28, 1874:

> In a little while, there will be a concourse of people in the streets. Methinks I hear someone inquiring, "What are all these people waiting for?" "Do you not know? He is to be buried today." "And who is that?" "It is Spurgeon." "What! The man that preached at the Tabernacle?" "Yes, he is to be buried today." That will happen very soon: and when you see my coffin carried to the silent grave I should like every one of you, whether converted or not, to be constrained to say, "He did earnestly urge us, in plain and simple language, not to put off the consideration of eternal things. He did entreat us to look to Christ."

We can imagine how scores who heard and remembered that impressive sermon, and who were among the vast crowds of mourners as the remains of the beloved pastor were being carried to God's green acre, blessed God for the prince of gospel preachers who never failed to declare the whole counsel of God. It is to be regretted that the predominantly evangelistic preaching Spurgeon was so notable for has passed out of fashion. The utterances from many a pulpit today would not save a sparrow. The Tabernacle never heard sermons on current events and politics or listened to essays on a hundred and one themes. Charles Haddon Spurgeon had only one theme he could ring the changes on in marvelous ways—Christ crucified, and His power to save all who looked to Him in faith! That was the message that filled the Tabernacle every Sunday with almost ten thousand people for well over thirty years, and it remains the only message that will fill churches today.

ABOUT THE AUTHOR

When Dr. Herbert Lockyer (1886–1984) was first deciding on a career, he considered becoming an actor. Tall and well-spoken, he seemed a natural for the theater. But the Lord had something better in mind. Instead of the stage, God called Herbert to the pulpit, where as a pastor, Bible teacher, and author of more than fifty books, he touched the hearts and lives of millions of people.

Dr. Lockyer held pastorates in Scotland and England for twenty-five years. As pastor of Leeds Road Baptist Church in Bradford, England, he became a leader in the Keswick Higher Life Movement, which emphasized the significance of living in the fullness of the Holy Spirit. This led to an invitation to speak at the Moody Bible Institute's fiftieth anniversary in 1936. His warm reception at that event led to his ministry in the United States. He received honorary degrees from both the Northwestern Evangelical Seminary and the International Academy in London.

In 1955, he returned to England, where he lived for many years. He then returned to the United States, where he spent the final years of his life in Colorado Springs, Colorado, with his son, the Rev. Herbert Lockyer Jr., a Presbyterian minister who became his editor.